Renewal

ALSO BY RABBI SHMULEY BOTEACH

The Michael Jackson Tapes
(PERSEUS BOOKS, 2009)

The Blessing of Enough
(SONY, THIS WORLD, 2009)

The Kosher Sutra
(HARPERONE, 2009)

The Broken American Male,
and How to Fix Him
(ST. MARTIN'S PRESS, 2008)

Shalom in the Home
(MEREDITH BOOKS, 2007)

Parenting with Fire: Lighting up the
Family with Passion and Inspiration
(PENGUIN PRESS, 2006)

10 Conversations You Need
to Have with Your Children
(HARPERCOLLINS, 2006)

Hating Women: America's Hostile
Campaign Against the Fairer Sex
(HARPERCOLLINS, 2005)

Face Your Fear: Living with
Courage in an Age of Caution
(ST. MARTIN'S PRESS, 2004)

The Private Adam:
Becoming a Hero in a Selfish Age
(HARPERCOLLINS, 2003)

Judaism for Everyone: Renewing Your
Life Through the Vibrant Lessons
of the Jewish Faith
(BASIC BOOKS, 2002)

Kosher Adultery: Seduce and
Sin with your Spouse
(ADAMS MEDIA, 2002)

Why Can't I Fall In Love?:
A 12-Step Program
(HARPERCOLLINS, 2001)

The Psychic and the Rabbi:
A Remarkable Correspondence
(SOURCEBOOKS, 2001)

Dating Secrets of
the Ten Commandments
(BROADWAY, 2000)

Kosher Emotions
(HODDER & STOUGHTON, 2000)

Kosher Sex: A Recipe for
Passion and Intimacy
(DOUBLEDAY, 1999)

Wrestling with the Divine
(JASON ARONSON, 1995)

Moses of Oxford: A Jewish
Vision of a University and
Its Life, Volumes One and Two
(ANDRE DEUTSCH, 1994)

Wisdom, Understanding, Knowledge
(JASON ARONSON, 1993)

The Wolf Shall Lie with the Lamb
(JASON ARONSON, 1993)

Dreams
(BASH PUBLICATIONS, 1991)

RENEWAL

A GUIDE TO THE VALUES-FILLED LIFE

RABBI SHMULEY BOTEACH

BASIC
BOOKS

A MEMBER OF THE PERSEUS BOOKS GROUP
New York

Books published by Basic Books are available at special discounts for
bulk purchases in the United States by corporations, institutions, and
other organizations. For more information, please contact the Special
Markets Department at the Perseus Books Group, 2300 Chestnut
Street, Suite 200, Philadelphia, PA 19103, or call (800) 810-4145, ext.
5000, or e-mail special.markets@perseusbooks.com.

Portions of this work were previously published in the book *Judaism for
Everyone*.

Designed by Timm Bryson

Library of Congress Cataloging-in-Publication Data
  Boteach, Shmuel.
  Renewal : a guide to the values-filled life / Shmuley Boteach.
    p. cm.
  ISBN 978-0-465-02045-4 (alk. paper)
  1. Jewish ethics. 2. Conduct of life. 3. Jewish way of life. 4. Self-
actualization (Psychology)—Religious aspects—Judaism. I. Title.
  BJ1285.2.B68 2010
  296.3'6—dc22
                                                              2010009367

10 9 8 7 6 5 4 3 2 1

To my parents-in-law,

SAM AND EVA FRIEDMAN,

*who lead lives of quiet virtue and exceptional communal devotion,
inspired and informed by Jewish values.*

*Thank you for tolerating me (I know it isn't easy) from the time
I was a rabbinical student in Sydney.*

Mostly, thank you for my wife. You did well, even if she didn't.

CONTENTS

TO LIVE ANEW

Many of us stagnate in lives that are going nowhere. We are either stuck in destructive patterns that undermine our happiness and snuff out our potential, or we run on a treadmill of routine that slowly kills off our dreams. In our hearts we know we are born for something higher, but by the time we hit our thirties and forties we have settled for a life that does not match our original expectations in any way. Then we tell ourselves that those long-ago visions of our future were never realistic in the first place. Mature people, we reason, adopt a more sober perspective. But the nagging sense that we deserve so much more never quite leaves us.

None of us are born thinking we are ordinary. Feeling special is an essential part of the human birthright. If you don't think you are special, you won't seek to contribute your gift to the world. But I meet people every day who seem content to throw away their days chasing money, watching TV, and accumulating as many possessions as possible. It's as if humans never evolved beyond the hunter-gatherer stage. We live in a culture where discussing the latest HBO series passes for stimulating dinner conversation. America has become a country of great contrasts: We're the wealthiest nation on earth and consume three-quarters of its antidepressants.

What happened to the feeling that we are special and the knowledge that special people don't waste their lives pursuing ordinary things?

Somewhere along the way that vital feeling of uniqueness died in us.

But it can be recaptured. What is needed is not another self-help book or personal empowerment seminar. We in the modern world do not suffer from a lack of motivation—most of us still get up in the morning and put in a full day's work. For the most part, we either are in a relationship or want to be in one. It's not that we're not *trying* to create a special life, but rather that we forgot what's important. We do not need a pep talk. We need a new vision of what truly matters, a new set of rules for how we should conduct our lives and to guide us in devoting our mental, intellectual, and emotional energies.

As a counselor, I have discovered that the principal cause of malaise is embracing the wrong values. Our culture never taught us what is truly precious, so we chased things that in the long run did not accord with our deepest desires.

Just think about the disparity between how you expend your daily energies versus how you wish to be eulogized one day. Does anyone want their rabbi, minister, priest, or imam to get up in front of the crowd that's gathered and launch into a discussion of the size of the house you lived in, or the luxury detailing of your BMW? Does anyone imagine they'll be most fondly remembered for how thin they were, or how much they exercised? Are there any among us so shallow as to want our legacy to be how many partners we bedded? And if not, why does the pursuit of these things drive us to endless distraction?

If your time is spent pursuing what doesn't accord with your deepest desires, you are living a lie—a sin against G-d, who gave you life so you could consecrate your existence to higher things. It is time to renew, recalibrate, and reorient our lives to focus on what matters.

This is not a self-help book. It is not a book that will teach you how to be an optimist or how to win friends. Even less so is it a book that tells you how to awaken your inner giant. No, this is a book about building a new life by rediscovering life's most precious values. In it you will discover a revolutionary take on the whole concept of values.

In this book I will reacquaint you with an eternal understanding of what in life is precious—and what thoughts, attitudes, and judgments we should run far, far away from. I'll introduce you to ancient values and their contemporary application. For those of you who are already familiar with the Bible's values, I hope you will find that the material presented here is fresh, even surprising.

I am a rabbi fully devoted to Judaism. But I do not observe my religion merely because it is the faith of my ancestors or because I want my children to embrace our tradition. Important as those things are, they are subordinate to something far more significant, namely, that my faith imparts to me a knowledge of life's infinite preciousness and potential. I don't want to throw my life away or dwell on stuff that's beneath me. From time to time we may all tell a lie, but living one is a different matter entirely.

I plan to turn some of your most cherished values upside down. While we think we know ancient values, we often have only a superficial understanding of the eternal truths embedded in them. For example, many people still believe in astrology and, by extension, fate. They believe their life was scripted before they were born. But nothing could be further from the truth. Fate is a myth designed to have us submit to forces beyond our control rather than bending those same forces to our will. It is profoundly disempowering. But in this book you will discover the Jewish value of destiny that can overpower your subservience to fate and the conventional life.

Another example is the belief in the value of education. Ever ask yourself why Americans today are more educated than ever before, and yet seemingly vastly more ignorant? For all of the college degrees we earn, we seem utterly unaware of the most basic facts of history, geography, and philosophy. Wisdom is in scarcer supply. That's because we should never have valued education in the first place. I know a number of people with PhDs who have completely messed up their lives. Likewise, nearly all the doctors who worked in Auschwitz were highly educated, but that didn't stop them from becoming some of the biggest monsters in history. We should pursue enlightenment, not education. Here you'll discover the difference between the two.

The same is true of salvation, one of the world's favorite values. Salvation is concerned with the state of your individual soul. Are you saved or are you lost? But is that what really matters, where you are going at life's end? Or is *redemption,* the contribution you make to the wider world here and now, more important?

We cannot keep fumbling in darkness only to wake up to how misguided our values were when we hit age sixty-four. It is time for us all to become more self-aware. Precious years are passing by, years that cannot be recovered.

Let's discover now what is truly valuable so we can live anew. This urgent truth applies collectively as much as it does individually.

The United States is suffering from a terminal deprecation of values. Greed has collapsed our economy and suffocated our spirit. Families scatter to the winds and divorce rates remain high. Our youth spend an average of eight hours a day disconnected from face-to-face interaction and real-life emotions. So where is the discussion of values that might reverse this societal decline?

Well, by way of a single example, the serious discussion of values that we so desperately need has been hijacked by the never-ending discussion about abortion and gay marriage.

For two decades I have watched these issues dominate the cultural debate on values. Whatever your views on gay marriage—whether you believe that gays should have the same rights as heterosexuals or you object to gay marriage on biblical grounds—one thing is for sure: The debate has nothing to do with imparting real values to our culture or saving the institution of marriage from certain destruction. We straight people don't need help from gays in destroying marriage, having done an admirable job of it ourselves, thank you very much. But so-called defenders of the sanctity of marriage and eternal values have chosen a convenient scapegoat.

Not even 10 percent of the American population is gay, but more than 50 percent of all marriages end in divorce. This was happening years *before* gays came out in significant numbers, let alone demanded the right to marry. In fact, the only men who seem to still want to get married in America are gays. While they are petitioning the Supreme Court to tie the knot, straight guys are breaking into a rash and running to the hills every time their live-in girlfriend of five years pushes for a ring on her finger.

The true cause of marital breakdown in our time is an absence of *real and substantive* values. We Americans are an ambitious lot. We want to succeed in everything we do. What we fear most in this country is being a failure, a "loser." But being a winner has come to mean having money, having power, and being famous. Where is the incentive to be a good man? The misguided values in our culture today encourage us all to have a career rather than a calling, to focus on our own ambition rather than cultivate our gifts to benefit other people. The only thing our young people learn about selfless love is that it is subordinate to unconstrained sexual pleasure, a funny, old-fashioned notion out of place in a ruthlessly efficient culture where *you* are always number one. We've redefined success to encompass only the professional sphere. In Hollywood, you can be on your fourth marriage and have all your kids in rehab, but so long as people are still paying $10 to see your movies, you're considered a success. On Wall Street, you can take the American taxpayer to the cleaners and pursue a life of endless womanizing, all fueled by gargantuan, government-facilitated bonuses, but as long as you drive a Ferrari and still occupy that $25 million Hampton estate, you'll still be welcome on the cocktail party circuit.

These are the rancid values being proffered to a nation that fought for freedom and became the world's first modern republic. More of the same is not going to help us rediscover our truest selves. We need a new set of values anchored in time-tested tradition.

Religion plays an indispensable part in this renewal—but not more of the same religion. As in the case above, with the extreme focus on gay marriage, we have arrived at a place of eroded values precisely because religion has, to an extent, lost its way.

Christianity in the United States generally comes in two forms. The first consists of the formal, mainline denominations, which tend to be more socially liberal and have either endorsed or tacitly embraced most secular values. The second is composed of the charismatic congregations who condemn the culture's mores and seem to delight in those judgments. Islam faces numerous problems as it confronts the modern world, including an aversion to democratic values and a rising number of fanatics who preach violence in G-d's name.

This is not to say that there isn't amazing good work being done by millions of Muslims and Christians the world over. On the contrary, the vast majority of the faithful are good people who stand up for what's right. It does mean that religion in our time is becoming divisive and is therefore compromising its own ability to positively influence the values discussion.

All of this points to the need for greater influence on the part of that other great world religion, the one that gave rise to both Christianity and Islam, and that's Judaism. Jewish values are uniquely suited to modern times.

Jewish values deliver a program for developing human potential that is suited to people of every spiritual persuasion. Forget the tragically mistaken notion that Judaism is only for Jews. Jews do not proselytize, it's true, believing that we must all, in the words of my friend Marianne Williamson, "honor our incarnation" and that the faith you were born to is the way G-d expects you to worship. But this was never supposed to imply that Jewish values weren't meant to influence all the earth's inhabitants, non-Jews included. Plenty of Westerners meditate and do yoga. That does not mean they intend to embrace an Eastern faith. Jewish values are universal.

After 3,300 years of near-exclusive practice by Jews, why do I say that in these times, the values I put forth in this book are for everyone? Because while Western society has figured out the answers to nearly all the great macrocosmic questions, it has failed utterly at the smaller ones. We know how to build skyscrapers, but a lasting marriage eludes us. We know how to launch satellites into space, but we are flummoxed when it comes to deepening our everyday interests beyond celebrity gossip. We can zap messages across the globe in nanoseconds, but we haven't yet overcome our addiction to the impulse purchase.

It is into this contradiction that Judaism fits in. Jews and Judaism have always focused on the small yet profound questions of existence. How does a man remain attracted to his wife for the duration of their marriage? How do families make special moments holy? How can we ensure that we are always honest in our commercial dealings? And how do we raise children who are motivated, respectful, and intellectually curious? It goes without saying that a failure to master these questions virtually guarantees an unhappy life.

Whatever our background, we all seek the same thing: happiness. But happiness is not something that, as Thomas Jefferson surmised in the Declaration of Independence, can be pursued. Rather, joy is the natural by-product of a life in harmony with G-dly values.

Every religion is known for certain characteristics: Christianity for its deep faith, Islam for its strong passion, Hinduism for its penetrating spirituality. Judaism stands alone not for its rejection of the divinity of Jesus or the prophecy of Mohammed, but for its singular concern with values. Most of the values the Jewish people bequeathed the world are no longer accredited to the Jews. Jews gave the world the one true G-d. Today the name is Jesus or Allah. The Hebrew Bible's idea that all men are created as equals today goes by the name democracy. Consider also the teaching of Leviticus 19:18, that one must love one's fellow man as oneself, is today called the Golden Rule and attributed to Jesus' Sermon on the Mount, though Moses proclaimed it thirteen centuries earlier.

Jewish ideas today come with the name Christianity, Islam, secular humanism, communism, utopianism, democracy, New Ageism, and even atheism and agnosticism. But there is a second tier of values—values that are wholly Jewish and that have not been embraced by the world, but that can bring great healing. They are, in acrostic form, DREAMSS, or *destiny, redemption, enlightenment, action, marriage, struggle,* and *sacred time.*

I touched on destiny and redemption above. And there are other Jewish values—as you'll discover as you read on. Judaism is not just a collection of arcane ideas. It is a program of action to ensure that G-dly values actually take root within our psyches and each successive generation. Jewish values take spiritual abstractions and translate them into a tangible reality inseparable from everyday life. Not every religious tradition appreciates that *values are useless unless they are ingrained into the human character.* We forget how easy it is for ideas and ethics to go out of fashion. Just fifty years ago, the Nazis trampled on all cherished values and almost succeeded in building a world based on darkness. All great ideas, as well as civilization itself, corrode with time.

The monumental values discussed here cannot remain like flowers cut off from their roots, for they will slowly wilt and die. I seek to promote the idea that the Jewish religion is a holistic set of inextricably linked values that together compose a state-of-the-art system for maximizing human potential. No other method of living has so celebrated life amid a history of death.

Long ago G-d gave the Jews a mission to spread light through G-dly values. It's time to hear that message again.

CHAPTER I

Destiny

∞∞∞∞∞∞∞∞∞∞

Life is either a daring adventure or nothing. To keep our faces toward change and behave like free spirits in the presence of fate is strength undefeatable.

—HELEN KELLER

I believe that you control your destiny, that you can be what you want to be. You can also stop and say, "No, I won't do it, I won't behave this way anymore."

—LEO BUSCAGLIA

Foremost among the threatened Jewish values is the idea of destiny. Destiny is the simple but radical idea that where you're going is far more important than where you've been. Destiny is both tremendously exciting and a tremendous burden. It means that you have to form a vision of your future. It also means you're forever forced to acknowledge that you have a choice.

Most people today no longer believe in choice, and science has been moving away from choice for decades. Do you have difficulty controlling your temper? It's in your genes, modern science says. We are told that we are genetically predisposed to certain behaviors and addictions and so have very little control over how these genes express themselves in our lives. Tempted to commit adultery? You cannot help it, evolutionary biology informs us, because men were designed to spread their genetic material as far and wide as possible. Evolution, especially—whatever its scientific merits—teaches us that we are more animal than human.

We see this denigration of choice in other domains as well. Sigmund Freud, one of the greatest thinkers of the twentieth century, encouraged us along this path when he posited that we are all masters of our mental household far less than we might suppose. Even Christianity doesn't entirely believe in choice. The Calvinist idea of predestination is pretty hostile to the idea of choice. And mainline Christianity maintains that only one choice really matters, and that's the choice you make about Jesus. You can lead a charitable life, be faithful in marriage, and provide thousands of people with secure jobs, but you are going to burn in hell unless you accept Christ's salvation.

The prevailing idea is simple: You can never rescue yourself. You are who you are. There's nothing *you* can do to elevate your station.

The ancient Greeks were not to be outdone in this department. They believed in something called fate, the precise opposite of destiny. Fate tells you that your point of origin is a mightier force in your life than your destination. The Greeks believed that everything that would ever happen to you had been decided before you were born. Every instant was preordained by the gods. That's why the Greeks excelled at tragedy—the essence of all the great Greek tragedies is that the hero or heroine is doomed to a sorry end because he or she cannot overcome his or her fate. Achilles took an arrow in the tendon of his heel. Odysseus was compelled to spend years of wandering after the Trojan War. The gods needed entertainment, and so they pushed you around like a piece on a game board. You were a stock character in a melodrama you had no hand in writing.

The siren song of fate lingers still. Popular astrology says that your character traits, as well as the kind of romantic partner you're compatible with, were shaped by the positions of the stars on the date and hour you were born. The moral of the zodiac is that you are so insignificant, and the choices you make are of so little consequence, that giant balls of gas hovering thousands of miles away have more power over your heart and mind than you do. What's even more astounding is that people seem to like this idea.

Fate is truly the most pervasive idea in the history of the world. Most of us cling to the idea of fate in one form or another, whether we express it or not. How many times have we heard social anthropologists say that poverty breeds violent crime? A very depressed man once said to me, "My grandparents are divorced. My parents are divorced. And now I'm getting divorced. It's fate. A family tradition!" The thought that he could break the tradition hadn't occurred to him. Or if it had, he'd dismissed it immediately.

Judaism completely rejects the belief that man is born doomed to a predetermined fate. Even more, Judaism rejects the idea that your past determines your future. Jews instead offered the world the most thrilling concept ever conceived, namely, that no human life is scripted and that each of us possesses freedom of choice. Sophocles may have stated, "Awful is the mysterious power of fate," and "Pray not at all, since there is no release for mortals from predestined calamity," but the Jew responded with the triumphant words of King David, "*Lo amus ki echyeh:* I shall not die for I shall live and speak the glory of G-d."

Judaism proclaimed that each and every one of us, regardless of our point of origin, can place a destination ahead of us—a vision of whom and where we want to be—and that by reaching that destination we transform fate into destiny. We proclaimed that what people make of their lives depends entirely on their actions. Notwithstanding modern behavioral sciences or genetic predisposition, the soul within us gives us infinite choice. We can always rise above circumstances. In every situation and in every predicament, we can choose.

This truth is embedded in the very beginnings of the Jewish faith. The father of the faith, Abraham, was a nobleman and very wealthy when G-d informed him that his children and his children's children would be slaves for four hundred years. G-d wanted Jews to begin at the bottom rung of the social ladder. Slaves are born to work, sweat, and keep their eyes to the ground. They concentrate on the task immediately at hand. They are not allowed to have dreams. Imagine Abraham's reaction to this news. I doubt he was thrilled.

The Jews started as slaves because the Jewish nation was going to teach the world that you could lift yourself up and set yourself free. Fate is where you start and conclude your life focused on your beginnings. But fate is a lie—that's the story of the Jewish exodus from Egypt. Destiny says your destination is what matters. *That* is what distinguishes you. Destiny is the truth. You are not an animal, subject to instincts, reflexes, and forces beyond your control. Your life is unscripted.

All Negro spirituals draw inspiration from Jewish history, from our path from slavery to emancipation. As Martin Luther King Jr. said in a famous speech in Detroit, segregation was guaranteed to suffer defeat "because it is nothing but a new form of slavery covered up with certain niceties of complexity." His religion had revealed to the black man "that figuratively speaking, every man from a bass-black to a treble-white is significant on G-d's keyboard." In that truth, King glimpsed both his and his people's destiny.

Long before the Civil Rights Act was passed, King declared, "In a real sense, we are through with segregation now, henceforth, and forevermore." What was his inspiration? He referenced it in the beginning of the lecture he gave in Memphis, the night before he died: Moses standing in Pharaoh's court centuries ago and crying, "Let my people go."

It is hard to underestimate the impact of this orientation. "The Patriarchic Covenant introduced a new concept into history," wrote Rabbi Joseph Soloveitchik. "While universal (non-Jewish) history is governed by causality, by what preceded, covenantal (Jewish) history is shaped by destiny, by a goal set in the future." Most historians work from the assumption that what *has* happened determines what *will* happen. But Jewish history is pulled, as if by a magnet, toward a glorious destiny.

In his 1946 book *Man's Search for Meaning,* Holocaust survivor Victor Frankl gave the definitive rebuttal to the belief that we are nothing beyond creatures of our environment. He observed concentration camp inmates living in barbaric conditions and emerged with evidence that fate was an illusion. "We who lived in concentration camps can remember the men who walked through the huts comforting others, giving away their last piece of bread. They may have been few in number, but they offer sufficient proof that everything can be taken from a man but one thing: the last of the human freedoms—to choose one's attitude in any given set of circumstances, to choose one's own way."

Frankl's unforgettable point is that even in the depths of hell in Auschwitz, he still possessed the capacity to choose. The Nazis had robbed him of his physical freedom by incarcerating him in a camp. They had stolen his human dignity by forcing him to defecate in public. They had robbed him of joy by murdering his closest kin, and they had robbed him of his uniqueness by reducing him to the number tattooed on his arm. But one freedom they could never wrest away: the freedom to choose how he would react to the humiliations and horrors being visited upon him. *Everything can be taken from a man but one thing: the last of the human freedoms—to choose one's attitude in any given set of circumstances, to choose one's own way.* That a Jewish prisoner in a Nazi death camp can still claim to be free is the ultimate testament to our ability to write our own scripts. No one can force another person to forfeit his or her own destiny.

You might wonder how this concept is relevant today. Sitting in a comfortable chair at Starbucks, sipping a latte, what does this have to do with your day-to-day life? You're not shackled in chains, you have not been imprisoned by murderous tyrants, and every time you fire up your Internet browser, you're presented with abundant options and opportunities.

The truth is that exercising our freedom to choose—and understanding the full implications of this freedom—remains a profound challenge for many people. Choice, of course, is often misunderstood. The Talmud maintains that forty days before a child is born, an angel named Azariel announces whether it will be male or female, rich or poor, to whom he or she will be married, and how long the child will live. Isn't this a contradiction? In fact, this is the Talmud's way of saying that the choice left to us humans is limited. No one consults us on whether we wish to be born, to whom we are born, what gender we will be, or what socioeconomic status we would prefer our parents to have. We have no say in any of these things, which determine so much else in life.

But Jewish values insist that we always have a choice in the most important thing of all, and that is whether to be good or bad. Everything else pales by comparison. Does it really make a difference if you're a street cleaner or the president of the United States, if as president you're impeached because you accepted a bribe? Would you not have been better off as an honest sanitation worker? Whom you marry is a major life choice. But how you decide to treat your spouse is a much bigger determinant of whether the two of you will be happy together. Your moral choices determine your character. Your sign on the zodiac is irrelevant.

No one can make you do something you don't want to do. If you want to do good, the choice is in your power. Likewise, if you want to lead a life of selfishness, no one can stop you.

By freedom of choice, Judaism means the capacity to exercise *moral* choice. Jewish values say that whereas people don't necessarily have the choice to do everything they wish—a man cannot choose to be as tall as a giraffe or to become a pumpkin—he does have the choice of how to *be*.

To complain or be content. To hoard or be generous and hospitable. To be good or be evil. There are no excuses. What you become is entirely in your own hands.

Once I confronted two brothers who had once been inseparable but had fallen out over a financial dispute. I beseeched the older of the two to apologize. "I simply can't. *He* was wrong and *he* should apologize," he said. "But that's not the point," I said. "What's more important—being right or having a brother? Here you have the opportunity to have your brother back. All it takes is a phone call. But you seem more interested in justice than sibling love, one of life's richest blessings. You are short-changing yourself for the sake of your pride." I shall never forget how he dialed his brother's home, but just as his call was answered, he put the phone down. "I want to do it!" he told me. "But I can't." He was imprisoned by his own stubbornness and fixated on the past. He refused to acknowledge his freedom to choose a different destination for himself and his brother.

The choices that confront us every minute of every day are totally undetermined. A kid growing up in a slum may have little immediate opportunity to improve his economic situation. But he can choose how he will respond to his poverty. Will he take drugs and mug passersby, or will he try to earn a decent living? Will a child growing up in such squalor choose to blame the rest of humanity for his lack of privilege, or will he try to overcome the challenges imposed upon him and practice love for others? Will the child who is born in a Fifth Avenue penthouse be conceited, condescending, and arrogant, indulging his every immoral desire and exploiting those lower on the social ladder, or will he share his wealth, practicing love and kindness?

Free will is what distinguishes us as humans. Divine unity within the cosmos is so complete that the only being that can rebel against G-d is, ironically, the one who was created in His image. Animals are ruled by instinct and limited by nature. They cannot transcend their biological programming. Ten thousand years from now, lions will still prey on zebras, and beavers will still be building dams. Both are predictable creatures. Only humans were empowered by the Creator with the ability to shape their natures and defy the divine will. Free will makes possible right and wrong, meaning and nothingness. Free will grants significance to our actions and unique dignity to our human existence. Free will enables our destinies.

The ancient rabbis note that after each of the first five days of creation, the Bible says, "And G-d saw . . . and it was good." On the sixth day, the day of Adam's creation, the wording changes slightly: "And G-d saw . . . it was very good." What changed so that on Friday it was *very* good? The rabbis answer that it was precisely the fact that on Friday man was endowed with an "evil inclination," a selfish impulse! It was the desire to be bad, to rebel against G-d, the drive for base physicality, meaninglessness, and a world devoid of G-d's presence.

But how could the "evil inclination," the source of all sorrow, be "very good"? The answer, of course, is that it is only the option of moving away from G-d that makes meaningful our choice to cleave from Him.

The story of Adam is that of human existence par excellence. Like Adam, we stand before our creator, choosing our response to the divine command. This is the true meaning of "the image of G-d." We, like G-d, are free.

Destiny means that your life will go where you take it. This is a powerful and terrifying proposition. People take a certain comfort in thinking they can't control their destiny. It provides a nice gloss on some of our shortcomings and failures. Can't get into Harvard? Nothing to do with my GPA, you can say—it wasn't meant to be! Can't lose weight? Well, look at my parents, you say, I was practically born with a tub of buttered popcorn in my hand.

The idea that you are a car and not a train, stuck to a set track, is terrifying, because car accidents happen every day. We all know people who've reached a certain age only to find that their lives are a jumble of broken relationships, stalled opportunities, and self-destructive habits.

It is absolutely horrifying to contemplate the idea that they are solely responsible—which is why most people reject it.

Freedom is indeed a terrible responsibility. Booker T. Washington was a freed slave, and in his writing, he vividly describes the day Union soldiers came to his plantation in the South. He depicts a scene of jumping and ecstasy and rejoicing that lasted for about fifteen minutes. Then, as Washington tells it, a cloud of moroseness descended. The newly freed slaves moved back to their homes in silence. They had realized something: Before this moment, all decisions had been made for them. They'd had no choices. Now life would be different.

Throughout history, people have wanted plenty of other Jewish values but have avoided this one. Why? It's an important question. Pundits and political analysts routinely debate whether people really want to be free. When America goes into Iraq and forcefully liberates its citizens, is that a good thing? Do 400 million Arabs really want to be free? Or is it America that is imposing its values on a region vastly different to it? Was the second Iraq war, as many observers in Europe alleged, simply American imperialism and hubris? Before the war started going badly, many said that *of course* people wanted freedom. We'd done this before and it had worked. After WWII, Americans forced democratic elections in Japan and Germany, both of which are now flourishing economies and open societies. John F. Kennedy, in his 1961 inaugural address, promised that we would "pay any price, bear any burden, meet any hardship, support any friend, oppose any foe, in order to assure the survival and the success of liberty." George W. Bush said something similar in his 2005 inaugural: "The best hope for peace in our world is the expansion of freedom in all the world."

But when the situation in Iraq didn't improve, many of freedom's earlier cheerleaders said, *Look, maybe we were mistaken. Some people don't want to be free.* Who's right? In his groundbreaking book *Escape from Freedom*, Freud disciple Erich Fromm essentially alleges that most people feel paralyzed by choice. They like it when someone makes decisions for them.

They're content to let the people of New Hampshire and Iowa decide the outcome of our national elections, or let fashion magazines tell them what to wear. Fromm argues that people don't want to be free, and that's why Christianity is so popular. In Christianity, it matters only that you embrace Christ. Why is Judaism comparatively less popular? Because people don't like to choose. Judaism says that you'll always be accountable for what you choose and your life will be determined by one thing and one thing only: the choices you make.

I loved Francis Fukuyama's book *The End of History and the Last Man*, in which he argues that once people taste freedom, they can never return to shackles. As King said, "The yearning for freedom eventually manifests itself." Democracy is the end of history, Fukuyama writes. It can't be improved upon and it can't be replaced. But that was in 1992. When I heard Fukuyama address a conference in Mexico more recently, he seemed to retreat. People in Russia seemed to be wary of democracy, he said. And then there was China, which seems to have a flourishing economy without democratic institutions. I approached Fukuyama afterward and expressed my disappointment. He agreed that we needed to shore up the value of freedom and human empowerment, and not undermine it, but still he seemed concerned about its prospects.

Freedom requires eternal vigilance, which is why it's one of the most important Jewish values. The Jews communicated to the world the belief that we are all capable, indeed obligated, to make tomorrow better than today.

Could Iraq have another Saddam Hussein? I think not. Once you get used to even the terrors of freedom, as opposed to the terrors of having no freedom, there is no going back. We see this in our own history. Think of the American colonists. Our country was founded on the great and noble principle of freedom. But think of how it came about. What was the overwhelming oppression the British brought to American shores? They taxed us! (A little. The taxes we pay today are much higher, and the income tax as we know it wasn't instituted until the twentieth century.)

The truth is that the British treated us, comparatively, pretty well. Even the Boston Massacre was hardly to the scale of what normally gets called a massacre. Six people died, as opposed to the hundreds who can be killed in a single suicide bombing. I don't mean to sound glib or minimize that event's gravity, which was of course horrible and tragic, but I do want to make a point: We simply didn't like Britain's intermittent oversight. We were far away from British shores and had become used to doing what we wanted to do.

There are a couple of theories as to why Jews are successful. One is that Jews are smarter than other people. That's a racist notion that none of us are going to endorse. Michael Steinhardt, a prominent Jewish philanthropist and a dear friend, told me he might agree with academics who argue that it's a matter of social Darwinism. The idea is that all the dumb Jews were killed off—the halfwits were impaled by Cossacks, while those who were smart enough managed to elude impalement. But this account doesn't hold water. We were the one community that had structures in place to keep the dumb ones alive! We had special dowries for poor brides, and special orphanages. Judaism has a tradition of giving its weaker members the resources to live.

So survival of the Jewish fittest isn't the reason why 25 percent of the world's Nobel Prize winners, and almost 50 percent of Pulitzer Prize winners, have been Jewish. Why are Jews so successful and prominent when we're not even 1 percent of the world's population? I believe it's because of our belief in destiny, the idea that what we do will determine what we become. Destiny is the single most empowering idea in all human history.

That's why it's the first of all Jewish values. The name "Israel" means he who struggles, literally he who wrestles with G-d. We wrestled with fate. We wrestled even with G-d's plan. In the history of the world, which people have dared to take on G-d? For me, the most inspiring story of the entire Bible is that of Moses in the wake of the Jewish sin of the golden calf. After smashing the two tablets of the law into a thousand pieces, Moses again ascended Mount Sinai for forty days and forty nights to convince G-d to reverse His decision to destroy the Jews before they could enter the Promised Land. Moses pleaded so hard that he became physically ill. He coughed up blood, but he would not relent. When G-d still wouldn't forgive the Jews, Moses offered a statement that easily passes as the greatest expression of chutzpah ever. "Now, if you will forgive the people," Moses said, "then good, but if you will not forgive their sin . . . blot me out, I pray you, from the Torah which you have written." You must forgive, he said. If you don't, please remove my name from the Torah. I don't even want to be mentioned in that book of yours.

G-d said: "These people will die." Moses replied: "No. They *are* going to get to the Promised Land." I find it the most beautiful defense of human life ever recorded.

But we're supposed to submit to G-d's plan, right? Isn't that what all great religions tell us? Islam and Christianity agree on this point. The Jews, however, say that you have to fight. You have to wrestle to fulfill your destiny.

If you accept that you always have a choice, there's no excuse for what you didn't become in life. There's a famous story about Reb Zusha. He is on his deathbed, surrounded by thousands of students, and he's crying. "Why are you crying?" they ask him. He was a respected man and had lived a virtuous, honorable life. "I'm about to come before the master of the universe," Reb Zusha said, "and he's going to ask me, 'Why weren't you as great as Abraham?' And I'll say, 'G-d, you didn't create me to be Abraham.' Then G-d will say, 'Well, how about King David?' 'But G-d,' I'll say, 'I wasn't King David.' 'What about Maimonides?' G-d will ask. Again, no. Then G-d will say, 'Zusha. Why didn't you become Zusha?' And then I will have nothing to say."

Who could have predicted that three years after the Holocaust, the Jewish people would create their homeland and found the state of Israel? This is incredible. One out of every three Jews alive was killed in the Holocaust. The historical precedents for people so afflicted were not encouraging. The Romans were chased off by the barbarians and never heard from again. But the Jews, with no armies, no guns, and no soldiers, a mere *three years* after unspeakable atrocities were leveled at them, built their own country.

What's the difference? The Romans believed in fate. They would go to oracles and ask to be told what lay ahead for them. But the Jews believed in destiny. Eighteen times a day, they would pray for a return to Israel. This value is so strong, so potent, that even the crematoria of Auschwitz could not extinguish it.

There is a time in each of our lives when we open our eyes and discover that rather than controlling our environment, we are allowing ourselves to be shaped by external events. As a rabbi and counselor, I have long noticed that the principal emotion that governs people in their advanced years is regret. The Talmud says that most men and women realize only a fraction of their ambitions.

It is depressing to reach midlife, look into a mirror, and discover that we've arrived at an unwanted destination. People often see themselves repeating the very patterns that disillusioned them about their own parents. I remember promising myself on countless occasions that I would not make the same mistakes my parents made that undermined their marriage. Now every time I find myself becoming upset over a trifle and unable for a short time to overcome my annoyance, I acknowledge just how imprisoned I am.

But it is that confrontation with my incarceration that inspires me to struggle to break free and to approach my wife and apologize if my behavior has been inconsiderate. I have no desire to live my life as a prisoner.

CHAPTER 2

Redemption

∞∞∞∞∞∞∞∞∞∞

*Social improvement is attained more readily by a
concern with the quality of results than with the
purity of motives.*

—ERIC HOFFER

*Hell is yourself and the only redemption is when a
person puts himself aside to feel deeply for another
person.*

—TENNESSEE WILLIAMS

What is the source of human hope? Why do we believe that tomorrow will be better than today? Just look at human history.
It's a long story of constant war and fatal disease. Nations don't seem to
get along and human life is chronically vulnerable. Even today, when standards of living have greatly increased, there is still great unhappiness.

So what gives us the faith that we can cure AIDS, cancer, and obesity?
Every time we cure one disease, another pops up. What makes us imagine
we can rid our streets of drugs and criminals? No one has succeeded in

ridding the world of these ills in the past, yet we persist in speaking as if progress is within our reach.

This hope springs from the value of redemption. Where Christianity speaks of personal salvation, Judaism counters with world redemption. For Jews the focus is not on whether we go to heaven and how to get there. Yes, we do believe in the afterlife, but there is precious little discussion of the topic in Jewish texts. We don't much care for the next world. We are focused on this one.

Salvation appeals to those for whom this world is a place of endless pain. It promises a perfect world in the hereafter where one lives in utter bliss for all eternity. I can't help but feel this is a bit of a cop-out. I would rather try to bring a little heaven down here to earth, so that this life holds rewards for current and future generations.

In Jewish values, the concern is not where you personally are going when you die, but the impact you make on this world *before* you die. Once, in a public debate, a Christian scholar who is a close friend asked me how I could be sure I was going to heaven. "Unless you believe in Jesus," he said, "you simply don't know." I paused and then said, "To be honest, I couldn't care less where I'm going. That's just a selfish consideration. Heaven, hell—who cares? As a Jew I rarely think about it. My greater concern is: *Does my life matter down here, and am I a blessing to others?*"

Here you see radically different understandings over a concept central to both religions, the Messiah. For Christians, the Messiah is the road to heaven. Belief in Jesus is asserted as the means to a blessed afterlife. For Jews, the Messiah is the belief that humans can make the earth better. It's a belief in forward progress, and in humankind's ability to improve the world. The Christian Messiah is an otherworldly concept whose primary purpose is forgiving sin. But the Jewish messianic vision is about redeeming the here and now.

Let me put the contrast even more bluntly: Don't believe for one moment that if your marriage sucks in this world, it's going to get better in the next. That kind of thinking, which feeds off a fantasy of the future instead of mastering today, has brought religion into disrepute. Yes, I do believe in the world to come. But for us Jews, it's this world that will be perfected in the messianic era. When a soul dies, it ascends to heaven only as a way station. It is ultimately coming back to earth at a time of human perfection.

Let me also ask a question. For all those who can't wait to get to heaven, do you really believe there will be any delight there that is greater than the delight you take in your children? Can you imagine a love there deeper than what you once experienced with your spouse?

Heaven is here. It is waiting for us to grab it. Yes, there is a heaven above. But it still can't compare to the heaven we can create down here.

The Jewish idea of the Messiah is the engine for all human advances, and the sustainer of all human dreams. It's the basis of the value of redemption. Messianic expectations and the promises of utopia have permeated society as well as the way we—both religious and secular individuals—imagine our future. The Messiah is the essential motif behind nearly every Hollywood action movie. One good guy, however imperfect, such as James Bond or Dirty Harry, battles against corruption and redeems the world from oblivion.

Messianism states that the world began at a fixed point—creation—and will improve until it reaches a glorious climax in the form of a world devoid of war, disease, and hunger. This perfect world is a joint partnership between the Almighty and man. According to Isaiah 32:15–17: "Until a spirit from on high is poured upon us, and the wilderness becomes a fruitful field, and the fruitful field is deemed a forest. Then justice will dwell in the wilderness, and righteousness abide in the fruitful field. The effect of righteousness will be peace, and the result of righteousness, quietness and trust forever."

We humans need to do all we can in promoting justice, finding cures, developing agriculture, and spreading wealth. G-d will add the finishing touches to what lies outside our ability.

This Jewish value of redemption is also known as linear history. The religions of the East believe in cyclical history, an endless cycle of creation, destruction, and reincarnation. This explains why Eastern religions are so meditative in nature. They focus on elevating the inner self rather than bettering the outside world. If the universe is cyclical and all that is built is destined for destruction, then human effort ought to be directed at perfecting the life of the spirit rather than the ephemeral life of the body.

But the belief that history is linear rests on the idea that human effort to perfect the world is never wasted. Rather, every human undertaking in each generation is cumulative until a critical mass is reached and G-d redeems the world of the last imperfections that lie outside human capability. Whereas cyclical history emphasizes spiritual enlightenment, linear history leads to building hospitals and paving roads.

The Jewish idea of redemption contrasted sharply with the cyclical orientation that dominated the ancient world. Babylon offered a stagnant worldview in which history recounted man's vacillation between two opposing forces. The ancient Greeks wrote of fate, positing that all hope was futile since humans could not overcome their predetermined end. But the Jews advocated a doctrine of free will and social progress that rejected the idea that we were condemned to an endless cycle of repetition. It asserted that notwithstanding all evidence to the contrary, the story of man is one of progress and refinement.

Can you imagine if Jewish ideas of redemption and messianic progress had never took hold in the world? You would get married, the passion would begin to wear off, and you would believe that it could never fire up again. Your relationship with your teenage kids would be reduced to monosyllables, and you would have no hope of ever enjoying a loving relationship with them again. You'd go bankrupt and never believe that you could recover.

The second law of thermodynamics is that of entropy increase, which states that the world naturally progresses from order to disorder. Energy gradually becomes more diffuse and unusable. In personal and biological terms, the body naturally breaks down, starting sometime in our mid-twenties. These are physical facts. But Jewish values reject the inevitability of decay in every other realm of human experience. We build, we hope, we progress. Human will *can* overcome and reverse the natural inclination to disorder.

But far more than simply a comfort through the darkest periods of Jewish history, the prophets' vision has served as inspiration for human hope, prayers, and action everywhere. It has rubbed off on all nations and everyone working to repair the world. What else could have inspired warring countries to come together in San Francisco in April 1945 to form the United Nations? Those that convened were still in the midst of fighting the worst war the world had ever seen, replete with genocide and the slaughter of millions of innocents, including 6 million Jews. What made the nations that sent delegates believe they could establish global cooperation and bring an end to war? Did they not realize that combat was inevitable in a world of limited resources? Any student of history can tell you that war is endemic to mankind. Yet these nations assembled to create global peace, ignoring all lessons of history.

On the Wall of Peace at UN headquarters in New York, verses from Isaiah are etched in stone: "And they shall beat their swords into plowshares and their spears into pruning hooks. Nation shall not lift up sword against nation, neither shall they learn war anymore." The creators of the UN were guided by the messianic prophecies of the past that foretold a peaceful future. Redemption is the inextinguishable candle of hope flickering within the most palpable darkness. It is the eternal ray of sunlight that Judaism has bequeathed the world.

The imminent promise of a world filled with light has nagged at the Jews constantly. How else to explain why people who have suffered so much are so optimistic, and dedicate so much of their creative talent to social progress?

Jews are the progenitors of many of the world's "isms"—such as secular humanism and communism—because they are always searching for a utopia. Yes, many "isms" brought tyranny and destruction, based as they were on the false idea that humans can create a utopia without G-d's guiding hand. But however errant the effort has sometimes been, Jews will not make peace with suffering. They constantly seek to return to their promised land, and when that is not possible, they will build a new promised land.

But what does the value of redemption mean on a *personal* level? I have found that audiences wrestle with this question, mostly because they're confused about the concept itself. Redemption does *not* entail being restored to a previous incarnation of yourself, one not blighted by sin or regret or decay. Redemption does not mean returning to a more innocent and simple life. Redemption is when you, wiser from experience and accountable for all that you've learned, devote yourself to nurturing G-d's world—*not* yourself. Redemption happens when you decide that being a blessing to others is more important than repairing yourself.

It's no surprise that embracing the value of redemption has consequences in every area of life. The first involves how we make ethical decisions. Consider this question: Should you do the right thing for the wrong reasons? Say a man comes to a community and announces that he's a very wealthy man and that he has an idea. "I want to build a giant orphanage. I would build it myself, and pay for it all," he says. "But what's stopping me is the knowledge that I don't care. I'd be doing it just because I want my name on all the lists of the city's fat-cat philanthropists. I also want to wash my hands of some questionable business dealings I got tangled up in earlier in my career. Plus I want my name chiseled in stone."

What would you say? The man has admitted that he's egotistical, even borderline megalomaniacal, and that his desire to help is insincere. He may even be cruel.

Or say that you're a guy and you meet a pretty woman who asks to use your cell phone. She needs to make a quick call to leave a message for a friend. So you lend her your phone for five minutes because you're hoping that she'll then agree to have dinner with you and who knows what else. Some say that if your motives are that impure, you're better off handing her some change and pointing her to the nearest pay phone.

Should you do the right thing for the wrong reasons? If your pretenses for taking action are false, are you better off sitting on your hands? Largely based on whether they privilege salvation or redemption, different religions present different answers to these quandaries. In Christianity, the emphasis is on me. *What is the state of my soul? If I do the right thing only because I hope to gain from it, and my heart is not engaged, I may become a worse person. My soul may be put in jeopardy because I'm misleading someone and possibly even myself.*

Then consider this: Has anyone ever heard a rabbi say that you need to think about where you're going to spend eternity? The reason Jews don't care about that question is that world redemption dictates that *those in need* are more important than *you*. To return to our man and the orphanage, here's what actually happened when the question was put to the founder of Chabad Hassidism, Rabbi Shneur Zalman of Liadi: The Rebbe said, "You may not mean it sincerely, but they with empty stomachs will eat very sincerely."

In other words, the impact you have on yourself shouldn't concern you much. What matters is the impact you have on others.

There is no worse hell than to be self-focused. It is bad enough to do it for a day, but for all eternity? If I went to heaven and sat there worrying about myself all day, to me that would be hell.

Which brings us to another consequence of embracing the value of redemption: You stop valuing perfection. We live in a culture that values perfection. In our political arena, we think our leaders must be perfect. They cannot be hypocrites. They can't espouse one virtue publicly and betray it privately. So when we discover that they have some flaws, we destroy good men and women who have served admirably.

We see this every four years when the media try to prove that leaders vying for national office are hypocrites. It's not enough for them to have excelled and shown true courage in one area of life. They need to be exceptional in all areas. John McCain refused to leave the Hanoi Hilton on a point of principle when offered release. Along comes the *New York Times* and insinuates that he's in bed with a lobbyist—literally. In the end the report was discredited. But what if it were true? Does that discount everything about him, or does it mean that while he has to repent for his actions he can still lead in other areas? Or let's say that Franklin Delano Roosevelt and his secretary, Lucy Rutherford, did carry on an extramarital relationship to the great anguish of Eleanor Roosevelt. Let's say it's all true. Ditto Thomas Jefferson and his slave Sally Hemings, and their six children. There's some indication that it was a loving relationship, but if Jefferson owned Hemings, how consensual could the sex have been? The Christian faith looks at this and says, how can this be? How are we to reconcile all these conflicting reports, and more important, how can we look up to these flawed people?

One more example: Martin Luther King Jr. reminded America that it had made a promise to uphold the principle that all people are created equal and that the country hadn't yet fulfilled that promise. I consider King one of the two or three greatest Americans of the twentieth century and I have endeavored to memorize his speeches. He has been one of my greatest lifelong inspirations and I am awed by the magnitude of his achievements at such a young age. After he died, his friend Ralph Abernathy divulged that King had committed adultery, and FBI recordings confirmed it. This made Abernathy a pariah—he'd betrayed a friend and tarnished the reputation of an American hero, making it harder for us to revere King as we once did.

How are we supposed to react to revelations that great men can be so flawed? If your emphasis is on personal salvation, poll numbers sink. Gary Hart was sunk by the revelation of his relationship with Donna Rice. But remember the Jewish reaction to Bill Clinton's infidelity? Most rabbis said that while his actions as a husband were deplorable, he did not have to resign as president. Why the indifference? Is it because Jews are immoral, callous, and have no sense of honor? Is it because they don't value marital fidelity?

I would propose another answer. Our Bible is exceptionally candid about its heroes' shortcomings. Abraham, Joseph, Moses, David—all flawed. How do we look up to these people? Why do we have to settle for such flawed men? Because our emphasis is not on personal salvation. Our emphasis is on world redemption. We care whether these men took the world forward to an era of peace and justice.

And even complete jerks are capable of furthering that goal. Even imperfect people can perfect the world. This means that no one should ever question whether to do the right thing, even just once, never to be repeated. Give a dollar to the guy begging on the street. Some will say, *What's the point? Give him a dollar and the next thing you know, 50,000 will be swarming around you, clamoring for more, and you'll never be able to keep up.*

I recently counseled a married couple who seemed trapped in destructive patterns. I said to the husband, you should apologize to your wife. He said, why should I? Tomorrow she would just find something else to blow up at him about. His apology wouldn't change a thing! I said to him, "But tomorrow has nothing to do with your obligation *this moment* to redeem the world, and especially your marriage, through the power of a single good deed."

Stop making meta-calculations. Don't stop yourself from doing what you know is right because you "don't mean it." Even if you're apologizing only because you simply don't want to fight any longer and even if you're still angry. Say it anyway because it's not about you. Apologizing draws people closer. One says "I'm sorry" because humility and a willingness to admit shortcomings are good things. Your feelings on the matter don't matter.

Redemption privileges relationships over purity. Professor Velvl Greene at Ben Gurion University in Israel tells a story about how he, a scientist and a secular man, came to befriend a rabbi in St. Paul, Minnesota, about forty years ago, who eventually took him to meet the Lubavitcher Rebbe in Crown Heights, Brooklyn. Soon after he and the Rebbe met, they got into a discussion about creationism, and the Rebbe gave Greene a famous paper he had written on the subject. Greene read it and found it ridiculous. So he wrote an eleven-page letter to the Rebbe that essentially told him to stick to what he knew and leave the scientific theorizing to more qualified people. It was an insulting letter. The next year he encountered the Rebbe in his office and worried about what he would say. But the Rebbe never mentioned it. The next year, same deal. Twelve years passed. By that time, Greene had become a religious Jew. Once again he met with the Rebbe and that time the Rebbe pulled out the letter, all eleven pages of vitriol and condescension.

"You sent this to me," the Rebbe began, "and I never responded. Can I talk to you about it?" The Rebbe, who had considerable scientific training, then proceeded to respond cogently, point by point, to the professor's scientific arguments. Greene was flabbergasted. "Why didn't you tell me this twelve years ago?" "Because we didn't know each other that well," the Rebbe said. "Because I would have won the argument and lost a friend. And I'm in the business of losing arguments and winning friends."

I tell this story to married couples who insist on standing on principle. I ask them, "What's better: being right or being divorced?" We all need to be willing to lose the argument and win the relationship.

Whenever you embrace the value of world redemption, you are suddenly free. You are free to develop your gifts without fear of being labeled a hypocrite. In contemporary mainstream culture, hypocrisy means you say one thing but practice another. So if some congressman says marriage is important but later he is revealed to be having trysts with strangers in public restrooms, he's branded a hypocrite. The public gets angry. In the Jewish worldview, he's not necessarily guilty of hypocrisy. When you preach something and don't believe it *even as you're preaching it,* you're saying it for ulterior motives, and *that's* hypocrisy. But if you firmly believe in the importance of family and then slip up and disappoint yours, that's something else. That's being inconsistent and weak. Yes, it is inexcusable. But it is understandable.

Why does this matter? Because people stop doing *good* things for fear of being labeled a hypocrite or worse. We love excusing ourselves from hard work and sacrifice.

Reb Zusha of Anipoli was a great Hassidic master and schoolteacher in Russia some 250 years ago. His daughter needed to marry so he sought out the fund for poor brides. The administrator of the fund gave him 500 rubles and, with a grateful heart, he began his journey back home. Along the way he detoured and came to a town he didn't recognize. Outside in the main square, a crowd had gathered. They were pouring water on a man who had fainted and someone was hollering about found money. Reb Zusha leaned over and asked what had just happened. "Well, this guy," his informant said, "he left his family for a year to work just so he could feed them. He comes back with 500 rubles and he goes to a store to buy toys for his kids and he puts the sack of money down for a moment and it's gone." Reb Zusha debated what to do. He excused himself for a moment, reached into his own sack of 500 rubles, extracted and pocketed 50 rubles, then rushed back to the crowd. "I found it!" he cried. Everyone rejoiced. Then they counted the money and found only 450 rubles. Reb Zusha was the thief all along, they decided! Days later a friend came to bail him out of jail. "Why didn't you tell them? Why couldn't you explain the situation?" he asked. The schoolteacher replied, "For once in my life, I wanted to do the right thing and take no credit for it."

Why is the world leery of the value of redemption? Because salvation feels so good. The whole world exists for you. Even Jesus died for you. It's an incredible thing to say that your understanding of G-d is the means to your ends!

In Judaism, the quintessential symbol is Abraham taking his son Isaac to be sacrificed. In the Jewish symbol, man dies for G-d. G-d does not die for man. When everything about you exists for G-d, that can be painful. It makes incredible demands. But for thousands of years, we Jews knew it wasn't about us, and that's why we're free. That is why we're still here.

Life is filled with pain and criticism and hardship. But when you live for others, you've turned those hardships into a blessing. *Now you know why you are here.* You are here to spread life and light and love. Earth is not just the antechamber until you get to a perfect world in heaven.

When a Jewish parent blesses his children on Yom Kippur, there are many things he or she can tell them to be: smart, wise, kind—all good traits any parent would want to see in their kids. This past year, I asked that my children might be a blessing to others, that they might provide uplift.

That is the question we ought to be asking ourselves: How can I make myself a blessing to others? One last story: A young university student went to Rabbi Manis Friedman seeking his advice. She had no friends, she told him, and no boyfriend. She was terribly lonely. She wanted to get married. Rabbi Friedman sent her to talk to the Rebbe. "I came all the way to ask you how I can change my circumstances," she told him. He looked at her and, after establishing that she was a student, told her to "always bring the salt and the butter" when she sat down at a table in the cafeteria.

Was the Rebbe speaking in riddles? She was whisked off before she could demand clarification. She was annoyed.

Later the Rebbe's words were explained to her. He'd said to her, *Don't you understand? You said you had no friends. You said, "I live for myself, and my light is trapped on the inside."* He encouraged her to go and be a blessing to others. When you're a blessing to people, they want to be around you, they want to laugh with you, they want to bring you to their home. *So if you're sitting down to eat, bring the water pitcher. Bring another person a fork. Bring the salt. Don't just think about yourself. You're doing it for you, but you're also doing it for others.*

Whenever you want something in your life, do it for someone else. If you stop worrying about you, you will let the light out. If you want to get married, think of who you can set your friends up with, because in so doing you increase the amount of love in the world.

You can never go wrong if you do right. If you have the opportunity to make other people feel as though they matter, by being the first to greet them, or by inviting them to a party, take the opportunity. We were placed on this earth not to worry about where we'll spend the next life but to make every man feel rich, to make every woman feel beautiful, to improve our collective experience not in the afterlife but here and now.

CHAPTER 3

Enlightenment

ᴏᴏᴏᴏᴏᴏᴏᴏᴏᴏᴏᴏᴏ

*A house is not a home unless it contains food and
fire for the mind as well as the body.*
—BENJAMIN FRANKLIN

Boredom slays more of existence than war.
—NORMAN MAILER

At the heart of the American experience is a profound paradox. Sixty percent of the population has a college degree. We are one of the most broadly educated peoples of all time. On the other hand, we manifest abysmal ignorance. According to a 2006 National Geographic survey, 63 percent of Americans ages eighteen to twenty-four couldn't locate Iraq on a map, despite nearly constant news coverage since the war began in 2003. Seventy percent could not find Israel on a map of the Middle East.

We're also reading less. In a poll taken in 1982, about 60 percent of young people reported reading literature like books. By 2002, that number had dropped to just over 40 percent. Go on an airplane. You'll see scores of people staring at the seat in front of them rather than reading a book. We've reached levels of ignorance that would be comical if they weren't so tragic. Look at the way expletives have come to assume so many varied meanings today, the way cuss words are used to connote human emotions. Even the benign word "thing" is overused. Remember George H. W. Bush saying, "I'm not good at the vision *thing*"?

I don't expect our politicians to be trained in the ways of parliamentary debate. But to use the word "thing" for every*thing* has consequences. It means we are communicating within a very narrow range of expression. And failures in language can lead to failures in thought as well as melt-downs in relationships. The phrase "you don't love me," for example, plagues all marital disagreements. A husband doesn't thank his wife for dinner, and she thinks and says, "You don't love me." A husband works hard, comes home, and isn't greeted or embraced by his distracted wife, and he thinks, "You don't love me." People often don't have the words to say what they really feel. We say we "love" ice cream, but we also "love" our spouses—the exact same word for rather different sensations. When we can't express ourselves precisely, important distinctions and nuances are lost.

I bring up the consequences of ignorance to illustrate the importance of the next Jewish value, and that's enlightenment. The world values education, and that's where we went wrong. An education is a means to an end. It's the method by which people get degrees and careers. It treats the acquisition of knowledge not as the satisfaction of an insatiable curiosity but rather as a path for future success. And it explains why so many people today learn so much and know so little. They're driven by the pursuit of status rather than the pursuit of knowledge. So they'll make do with knowing just enough to get by and no more.

Often, intellectual curiosity decreases the more formal education one gets. I've seen this with my kids—they used to read so many books. They had a real passion for reading. But as they got older, they started reading less for fun. Their schools had made knowledge a chore. The more homework they did—and these days it seems endless—the more they associated reading with work. We cram kids with so much information that it ends up coming at the expense of their intellectual curiosity. When the acquisition of knowledge was something organic and fun, my kids loved reading. But the moment it became tedious and laborious, the fun disappeared. The subtler interests of the soul lost out to the constant testing of the brain.

Why do we do this? Because the notion that knowledge is worthwhile only so long as it advances your wealth is at the very core of our culture. The secular world stresses education so that learning will spur industry and research and thereby stimulate the economy. We've heard this from the likes of Bill Gates, who says that unless more American students focus on the sciences, Silicon Valley tomorrow won't be what it is today. "All knowledge should be practical and purposeful," wrote success guru Napoleon Hill in the perennially popular *Think and Grow Rich.* "Knowledge has no value except that which can be gained from its application toward some worthy end"—in this case, fattening your bank account.

This sounds like narcissism. To take a glorious thing like knowledge and subordinate it to yourself is to take something pure and corrode it with too much ego.

Jewish values dictate the opposite: Our career options are subordinate to knowledge. The Jews are called the people of the book. What an amazing term. If the purpose of knowledge is to *do* things, you would expect to have all kinds of people—the people of the pyramid, Internet, or dollar. To be the people of the book is to state that your highest aspiration is to know. As humans, we are obligated to be ennobled through intellectual adventure, to widen the horizons of the spirit by a lifelong quest to know. We are obligated to increase our appreciation for the complexities of the universe. This quest transforms us from superficial surveyors of the scene to sentient beings, fully awake to all of life.

This is why I tell my kids that I don't care that much about their grades. Grades are just one barometer of intellectual inquisitiveness, and even then, they're an unreliable instrument. Here's what I want to know: *Do you ask questions? Do you read books? Do you challenge your teachers? Do you just stare out the window?* What I want to know is that *they* want to know.

This is the secret of why Judaism insists on the never-ending pursuit of knowledge. Education is always given a utilitarian, and usually commercial, purpose. But enlightenment leads to a refinement of the self.

Now I say this with some hesitation, because plenty of societies that prized learning have proven capable of great barbarity. The book *Doctors Under Hitler* describes the intense professional training that physicians in Nazi Germany were forced to undergo. That premium on advancing knowledge certainly didn't lead to human refinement, so what's the critical difference? We don't simply pursue knowledge willy-nilly—but rather knowledge that leads to an understanding of values, of G-d, and of our obligations as human beings.

Enlightenment is a specific *kind* of knowledge. The Bible is all about how G-d makes demands on us humans. Immersion in scripture increases my sense of an obligation to humanity at large.

Enlightenment is also the surest hedge against boredom. By badgering our children to get good grades, we bore them. We give them the idea that once they've achieved their degree, they are done. The person who studies just to receive a degree will eventually, usually sooner rather than later, come to the conclusion that she knows all she needs to know and thus doesn't need to know any more. She can stop studying creation. This is the mistake of making knowledge a means to an end. It purges its pursuit of magic and becomes just another chore.

But the person who seeks enlightenment never stops studying, because there's no end to his or her curiosity. Curiosity is grafted onto that person. But those who don't have intellectual interests, those who are not curious, those for whom books are dull, who are addicted to visual stimuli and to sound effects, will be forever numb and unsatisfied. Boredom and ignorance are inextricably linked.

If you value enlightenment, you will never sit on a plane, staring straight ahead at the seat in front of you for five hours.

But why pick on boredom, you might ask. Isn't it harmless? I'll admit that boredom offends me even more than ignorance does. Boredom is one of the most corrosive trends in today's culture. The sheer vapidity of the stuff we consume in America to mitigate our boredom is astonishing. I remember being in England many years ago when the BBC and a handful of other stations were all that was on TV. Once I switched on the set in time to catch the beginning of a forty-five-minute program about an African fly. This TV program had no dialogue, no drama, no story. I watched in awe, wondering if we had really been reduced to such depths. Now I realize that program was positively Shakespearean compared to the absolute inanity of what we watch today.

There is a statement from the Talmud that I often quote to students and friends: A man's character can be tested in three ways: *be'kiso, be'koso, u've'kaaso.* First, "by his pocket" (is he a miser or is he generous?), "by his cup" (what does he say and do when alcohol has removed his inhibitions?), and "by his temper" (can he control his emotions when provoked?). Some add a fourth index of character: *af be'sahako,* "by his play" (Eruvin 65b). In other words, what activities does he choose to engage in when life doesn't compel him to act?

How one spends one's leisure time determines whom one becomes. Do you blow your time watching insipid television? Do you play solitaire on the computer half the day? Or do you read, spend time with friends, and make yourself and your talents available to others?

Sadly, many people are utterly flummoxed by the challenge of leisure. Give them a Sunday and they have no idea how to consecrate it to a higher pursuit. When they are not working or shopping or drinking, they are bored. Boredom is failing the challenge of leisure, and it leads to an erosion of meaning in life.

Boredom destroys our passion for everything. It even wrecks intimate relationships.

One man who understood this dynamic exceptionally well was Victor Frankl. In *Man's Search for Meaning*, Frankl wrote that there was a "kind of depression which afflicts people who become aware of the lack of content in their lives when the rush of the busy week is over and the void within themselves becomes manifest." Suicide, alcoholism, juvenile delinquency, a madness for money, even a rampant libido—all had roots in "the existential vacuum" and a "frustrated will to meaning."

The ancient rabbis acknowledged this existential vacuum and declared it to be the reason G-d gave man commandments after the flood in which the earth's evil inhabitants died. Boredom had led these people to sin, so G-d decided that it would be better for men and women to stay occupied with life-affirming and holy responsibilities.

Here's another intriguing lesson from the Talmud: If a woman marries a very rich man, and he's so rich that he tells her she doesn't need to work and that, in fact, she *shouldn't* work, this is grounds for divorce. Take Grace Kelly. She was a glamorous movie star and a working actress and then she married Prince Rainier of Monaco. He told her she must give up her career. It was beneath her dignity and his. By the Talmud's standards, this can lead to an oppressive marriage. Luckily the princess found her calling in philanthropy and community.

In another poignant example, the Talmudic sages ruled that the forced idleness of a housewife, either because the household had plenty of servants or because her husband prevented her from working, was unacceptable. Rabbi Eliezer maintained that even if a woman had a hundred maids, she ought to do some work in the household, "for idleness leads to *zimah*, unchastity." If the husband took a religious vow to abstain from benefiting from his wife's work, then he must divorce her and pay her dowry and settlement.

The reason: Idleness leads to boredom, which leads to feeblemindedness. Summing up the negative consequences of inactivity, the rabbis declared, "When there is nothing to do, you do what you ought not do."

What a radically different notion. Many of us aspire to a life of total leisure. But this is a profound mistake. It is oppressive *not* to work. When you don't have to work, when you have nothing to do, your mind wades into treacherous waters.

This is why we tell our kids not only what *not* to do but we also give them something *to do.* I remember distinctly the Lubavitcher Rebbe speaking one day to a crowded room. On his lap, one man held a two-year-old child who was waving around a set of keys. The kid clearly found the jangling noise delightful but it was very distracting to everyone else. Eventually the Rebbe interrupted his speech, looked at the boy's father, and said, "Give him something else to play with." He did not say, "Take away the keys," but that the child should be given something else to engage him. It was a simple statement but one that holds great wisdom.

Ignorance and boredom also lead to corruption. A bored culture is one that exploits women mercilessly. Why is there so much sexual licentiousness and vacuity on our college campuses? Why are kids and young adults drinking themselves into oblivion? One reason is they have so much time on their hands. When I was at yeshiva, we didn't have that kind of time. Even if we'd wanted to strip naked and pose for pictures for our campus newsletters (and as I recall it, that urge did not seem to grip us), the time simply wasn't there.

People need to have their energies and their higher faculties consumed not just by jobs and activities, however, but by something higher. Robert Nozick was a professor at Harvard University well known for his book *Anarchy, State, and Utopia.* He believed that war was mostly the product of boredom. War was not really the result of geopolitical tensions, but fundamentally the result of excess testosterone. Nozick said Pope Urban II started the Crusades, creating an enemy in the infidels in faraway lands, in order to give Christendom a great cause and in that way diverge pent-up energies from leading to mutual Christian annihilation. Once we start slaughtering other people, this thinking goes, the urge to slaughter one another will subside.

In other words, the cure for boredom was calculated destruction, because history had already shown that an excess of leisure time was disastrous. According to historian Edward Gibbon, ancient Rome disintegrated not through any external threat or power, but from the inside, and what destroyed it, in essence, was growing boredom. Slaves did all the work. Those who weren't slaves enjoyed public holidays every other day. The Romans tried to keep themselves busy with orgies and circuses and gladiatorial contests. All this was morally corrosive and slowly killed off the once robust Roman character until their empire became easy pickings.

Today, most Americans choose to deal with their boredom through acquisitions. If you're constantly buying new things, the thinking goes, you won't be bored. eBay has a market capitalization of $30 billion. It's the marketplace for all the stuff you bought when you were bored. It has the perfect business model for a bored generation.

The Jewish value of enlightenment offers a profound contrast. Judaism says that you can get bored only if you have a superficial personality. But if you are one of those rare people who understand that every life contains infinite depth, you will never succumb to boredom.

Virginia Woolf committed suicide when she was at the top of the world. An obscure short story written shortly before her death has remained largely unread. It's about a woman who one day is hit by a truck. Her grief-stricken husband ascends to the attic to look for mementos of their life together, and there finds green leather-bound diaries filled with his wife's handwriting. He starts to read. In these books, his wife refers repeatedly to "G," a man who was evidently important to her. The husband had never heard of "G"—"G" is definitely not *him*—and didn't even know she had a close connection to anyone else.

Then he discovers something more devastating. His wife had been depressed. All along he thought he knew her, but he had known nothing.

He didn't know what she did during the day, or what possessed her heart. The diaries describe her growing connection to "G" and how "G" ended his life when she refused to run off with him. The diaries conclude with the wife asking if she has the courage to make the same devastating choice. So her end in front of that truck was no accident. Bored as her husband was, he had never penetrated his wife's core and she had remained a virtual stranger to him, even as they shared a life for decades.

To cure boredom, you always have two possibilities. One is horizontal renewal. You put yourself at the center of an ever-expanding circle of possessions—a new car, new furniture, even travel. You earn money to escape your life. The other way is vertical renewal. You don't go outside but instead go deeper.

The essence of enlightenment is to know that everything has layers. That all people are fascinating. That you can scrape off the outer layer, and beneath that is another layer, and another.

Why is kabbalah so popular with celebrities? Why do people like Madonna and Ashton Kutcher embrace this strain of Jewish mysticism? The unique challenge of being a celebrity is that life becomes more boring for them more quickly than it does for the rest of us. Things happen quicker! We all aspire to walk the red carpet, fly first class, vacation in St. Bart's, but they've done it already. And they're bored! Having peaked, they have little new to look forward to. They turn to drugs to give life meaning and excitement. The kabbalah says that everything has a divine spark. Every fragment, every particle of the physical world is imbued with infinite light. The kabbalah tells restless people that if you dig deeper, you will find renewal. You won't have to get married for the ninth time or snort cocaine or bed hundreds of women.

Freud's father was a Talmudic scholar. Though many of his complexes have been repudiated, Freud did more than any other person in the twentieth century to further the belief that people have layers upon layers. He was the second most famous man on earth after Albert Einstein. He lived in a tiny apartment in Vienna. He didn't need to acquire property to keep himself entertained. Einstein himself lived at 130 Mercer Street in Princeton, New Jersey—an unimpressive little house. He was the smartest man since Newton, and he didn't even own a comb. He also didn't need things to make life eventful.

And because he wasn't bored, he wasn't arrogant. Bored people get an erotic thrill out of asserting their importance over others. Their lives require artificial drama to remain engaged.

But only knowledge creates true stimulation. Enlightenment makes life electrifying.

Better your kids go to a community college and love to read, and ask questions every time you bring a guest over to your house, than to have your kids go to Stanford and have no intellectual curiosity whatsoever. Better that they flunk a class than believe knowledge is just a means to an end. Knowledge has no end. It's a permanent means.

I have counseled many married couples in crisis. Many troubled marriages have a common denominator. A husband stops communicating with his wife because he thinks he knows her already. There is nothing new she can bring to the relationship. He has heard it all before. He stops making love to his wife. He knows every contour of her body, her every sexual response. He begins fantasizing about other women while making love to his wife, if they make love at all. Conversely, his wife stops asking him how his day was when he comes home. She knows what his day was like. It was the same as yesterday.

This lack of curiosity is what slowly makes them grow apart. That's why curiosity is arguably the most important ingredient in every happy marriage. The soul of marriage is to be curious about your spouse. If you're curious, you will always lean in to your partner to know him or her better. But if we've lost our curiosity toward someone, we no longer lean in to hear what they have to say. Our conversations start to dwell on practical matters, not intimate ones.

Similarly, the feeling of mastery destroys human relationships. When you think you've mastered something, you lose interest. You think, *Been there, done that.* True eroticism depends on obstacles. It relies on the frustration of desire. If you can't have what you want, even if it's only temporary, you keep on wanting.

That's why we need to develop a cult of curiosity. Too often we place pressure on our children to accumulate the signs of achievement rather than a love of learning for learning's sake. Consider this: The most successful people on the planet today are those who dropped out of college—Bill Gates, Steve Jobs, Paul Allen, Michael Dell, David Geffen, Steven Spielberg, Woody Allen. Why were these men successful? They were infinitely curious about how the world worked. It wasn't books that sparked their curiosity but life.

I often think of the insight shared by Rabbi Yitzchak Ginsberg, renowned kabbalist. It's about the biblical Ruth, a Gentile woman who marries a Jewish man. He dies, and Ruth is left in strange territory. One day she goes out to collect the wheat at a nearby estate. The master of the estate, Boaz, is kind to her, so Ruth asks him, "Why have you been kind to me, when I am a Gentile?" That, at least, is how her words are usually translated. Ginsberg maintained that the correct translation is: *How can you claim to know me, when I am unknowable?* In other words, don't condescend to pretend to know me. You know nothing about me.

The classic Jewish mystical text, the Zohar, says that the highest heights of knowledge are when you reach a point where you know what you don't know. Truly great masters of knowledge are those who admit their ignorance. In other words, they know what they *don't* know. They know what they *can't* know. We see this in physics. No matter how small the particle you discover, there's always something smaller.

Enlightenment keeps us humble. Socrates learned that the Oracle at Delphi had said he, Socrates, was the smartest man in Athens. Socrates laughed. So he set out on a search, asking questions, trying to determine if there was actually someone smarter than himself. He eventually decided that the Oracle was right. He, Socrates, was the only man prepared to admit his own ignorance. The more we know, the more we recognize our limitations. The more we recognize our limitations, the more sensitive we are to our fellow humans. TV shows end, even books end, but enlightenment is never-ending, ever alerting us to the infinite riches of G-d's creation.

CHAPTER 4

Action

○○○○○○○○○○○○○○○

*Remember, people will judge you by your actions,
not your intentions. You may have a heart of
gold—but so does a hard-boiled egg.*
—ANONYMOUS

*If our worship is inward only, with our hearts
and not our hats, something necessary is lacking.*
—LANCELOT ANDREWES

E ver heard of a non-believing Christian? An atheist Muslim? Probably not. Every religion is based on a belief.

Sometimes there's a set of beliefs, but usually one core belief animates
the whole. For Christians, that's Easter. Jesus died on Good Friday and
on Easter he was resurrected. His death atones for your sins. The central
doctrine of Christianity is that you're too flawed to save yourself and your
actions will never propel you into heaven.

Faith and submission, in other words, are the prerequisites for receiving
grace. Doing the right thing is not enough. People must first have the

right beliefs. And to escape eternal damnation, there's only one thing to do: believe in Jesus. You can give to charity, you can pray every day, you can be faithful to your wife every hour and every minute of a forty-year marriage, and you can devote every Thursday night to tutoring inner-city schoolchildren, all while raising three kind, talented, and loving children of your own, but all this is just icing on the cake. If you die without accepting Jesus as your savior, you are headed to the same place as the murderers, genocidal warriors, and Satanists. Faith ultimately trumps action.

In Judaism, we care far less about what you believe. What you do is more important. I've had about twenty debates with Dr. Michael Brown, a Jewish convert to Christianity who tries to convert Jews to Christianity. Mike and I have become friends through our very fierce debates, and our last public encounter was a debate on Isaiah 53. What emerged was that according to many Christians, a Jew who died at the hands of the Nazis would go to hell if he did not accept Christ as his redeemer. But if the Nazi, minutes before he died, accepted Christ as his savior, that Nazi would go to heaven. If you're a Jew who died without converting to Christianity, even though you moved mountains, then you will go to hell. Islam is not radically different—your pronouncement of faith is all-important.

The Jewish value of action requires something else from us. Arguably the most famous letter in the Jewish religion is Maimonides's *Iggeret ha-Shemad*, or the epistle of martyrdom. Maimonides lived with his family on the Iberian Peninsula when fanatical Muslims took over and tried to forcibly convert the natives. A venerated rabbi announced that the Iberian Jews had to accept death rather than let the words "there is no G-d but Allah and Mohammed is his prophet" cross their lips. Maimonides's letter absolutely eviscerated the rabbi's arguments. He wrote a scornful, devastating, scholarly letter that concluded with the suggestion that Jews should *not* follow the rabbi's instructions. If forced to choose between uttering the Islamic prayer and getting their throats slit, they should say the Islamic prayer.

I've studied this letter with my kids. They always ask, "Why was Maimonides so contemptuous? Why would he make the rabbi look foolish?" The answer is simple: Maimonides was afraid people would believe the rabbi and die as a result.

But the larger question is this: Why did Maimonides say it was okay for Jews to play along? Because they were being asked only to speak words, and because those words expressed only a statement of belief. In Judaism, action is far more important.

What does it mean to be a religion of action? I'll start with a story. When I was sixteen, I went to study in yeshiva in Jerusalem. We students would go out to public places on a Friday afternoon and encourage people to do a mitzvah, which roughly translates as a religiously motivated good deed. It was part of the Jewish outreach campaign practiced throughout the world by Chabad. We would go up to men and ask them, "Did you put the tefillin on today?" We would ask women, "Will you light the Shabbat candles today?" One day I approached an Israeli soldier and asked him, "Did you put tefillin on today?" Holding a pita in one hand, he looked at me, confused. He waved his right hand, with the pita, at me. "In this hand, I'm eating pork," he said. "Well, that's lucky," I said, "because we put tefillin on the left hand." And I pulled up his sleeve, put the tefillin on him, and said the prayers. There was no contradiction. Just because you're doing an act that is not in accordance with G-d's will doesn't mean you can't simultaneously do something that is. Every good action counts.

Here's another story. I was still a student but this time I was at the old Tel Aviv bus station with some other students. Right across the street from the station was an adult movie theater, and on its facade was an enormous mural of a naked woman. A guy who was no fan of the Lubavitchers walked over to me, mumbling angrily. "Look at this," he shouted as he approached, pointing at the mural. "This schmutz, it's disgusting! And here you are trying to talk people into doing mitzvahs in this filthy environment." I looked up at him and said, "Funny, I've been here two hours but did not notice the mural. You've been here five minutes and you seem obsessed with it." My point was that I was trying to do good deeds with people who knew very little about their tradition while he was saying that the environment counted more than the deed.

One more story. I was *still* a yeshiva student, and I got into a heated debate with another young student about the Chabad campaign. "Why do it?" he asked. "If you put the tefillin on someone and they don't believe in G-d, it's like putting tefillin on a monkey. You have to get people to believe in G-d first."

All of these people have a good case. Judaism is a religion, correct? It's not a corporation, not a sports game, not a theatrical production. You *believe* in G-d, right? To undertake an action when you don't believe in anything is absurd.

In this way of thinking, I see the legacy of the 1960s. Whether or not you lived through the 1960s, you've experienced one of the after effects of that period in history, and that's the elevation of all that is "authentic." If it's inauthentic, the thinking goes, it shouldn't be done. Your highest priority is to be true to what you're feeling at every moment, never to stifle your emotions because your emotions are what makes you, you.

I have several answers to this challenge. The first is a strong but incomplete answer. Say a marriage is dying from an absence of romance, and the husband comes to me and says, "Look, I don't feel those tingly, loving feelings for my wife anymore. We've drifted apart." Then I say to him, "Okay, that's understandable. But I want you to start giving your wife five compliments a day. Take her out to dinner. If she's good with the kids, thank her. Then I want you to take her shopping for clothes. Tell her what looks nice on her. Then I want you to share with her things that you don't like about yourself. Tell her how you feel about yourself."

The husband says, "But I told you—*I don't feel for her.* I don't feel any of this. That's the problem." But he agrees to this course of action anyhow. Within weeks he had started to fall in love with his wife again.

Why did this work? Because as I told the man, the more you do, the more you feel. The more love we demonstrate, the more love we will feel. Correct action is always superior to proper intention. Given enough time, the intention will follow.

What we do becomes an inextricable part of whom we are. Judaism is based on the idea that people can indeed change. They can be weaned away from narcissism and selfishness and practice honesty and sacrifice. We believe every person can gain control of his or her life.

But this change comes not through eloquent words, or from lofty thoughts, but through positive, repetitive action. Both Christianity and Judaism begin with the premise that humans can behave morally and become G-dly. But whereas Christianity argues that faith transforms the heart, Judaism maintains that inner transformation comes about only through external action. The hands fashion the heart. We learn to love people by acting sympathetically toward them even when we feel nothing.

Sometimes the heart is as cold as a stone. But while we can't always control our emotions, we can control our actions. And once we start behaving lovingly, our hearts respond to the action with genuine feeling.

Our culture likes to believe that emotions inspire actions. All Western romantic love operates on the assumption that the heart motivates the hands. But on some level, we know this to be false. A man may love his wife infinitely, but if he treats her badly, she'll walk. If you don't treat people with love, if you don't commit *loving acts,* then no matter what you feel, no matter whether your heart bleeds for them, they will not stick around. About 80 percent of husbands who cheat claim to love their wives. However, that love doesn't stop them from breaking their wives' hearts.

But I said that answer was incomplete. Let's keep going. Consider this: Every action embodies two dimensions. The first dimension is its motivation. The second is the action itself. Our culture is obsessed with motivation. But Jewish values maintain that as far as the consequences of our actions on the world at large are concerned, our motivation is of little consequence. The starving child in the Sudan who eats the bread we paid for rarely thinks about why we did it. The important thing is that he will live to see another day. It does not matter to a bereaved mother whether the drunk driver who killed her son had one too many because he was enjoying a romantic anniversary dinner with his wife or because he was at a frat party.

On the contrary, when it comes to perfecting the world, our motivation doesn't amount to a hill of beans. Nobody cares, nor should they.

The world is more important than us. Righteous action is more important than righteous motivation. If you want to succeed in a relationship, sure, your love and your affection matter. But even they are utterly secondary to doing the right thing.

So Judaism insists that one *must* do a good deed even if it stems from improper or insincere motivation. Refraining from doing a good deed because we question our intention is the piety of fools. The ancient rabbis taught that man's evil inclination is a wily fox, and it comes to us in many guises. Sometimes it dons the robes of the scholar and approaches us as an aged sage. "You can't help people when in your heart you know you are a hypocrite," the sage tells us. But this is a lie. Any rationalization that prevents us from doing a good deed emanates from the dark side of our personality. There are no exceptions.

This is especially true when it comes to charity. Nobody should give a damn why a philanthropist gives away his money. Perhaps he wants a plaque. Perhaps he wants to be knighted. Who cares? The poor still have a full stomach. Now imagine the opposite. A guy has tons of money but refrains from giving to charity because he fears he's doing it for the wrong reasons. How admirable is that? It sounds more like self-absorption to me.

My good friend Dennis Prager tells a story about a caller on his radio show. Joe was bereft, wracked with guilt. He explained that he was the sole financial and emotional support for his mother, who had been sick for years. At times, he said, "I wish she would succumb to her illness and die." Joe was ashamed of these thoughts and couldn't fathom sharing them with his siblings.

"Joe," Dennis told him, "you are one of the finest sons I've ever encountered." Joe begged not to be mocked. Hadn't Prager heard him? He said he wished his mother would die! But Prager was completely sincere. "You really take care of your mother? And your feelings are well hidden? Then you're a giant!"

It is how we act, not how we feel, that matters. It is *not* the thought that counts.

As I write this, there are 4,000 dead American soldiers in Iraq. I know that for all my saying that I support the troops, I don't actually do nearly enough. Who supports the troops? Those who enlist. Those who volunteer. Those who collect toys for soldiers' children. Those who organize fund raisers to support soldiers' widows and widowers. But the ones who weep while they watch the six o'clock news? Their feelings are irrelevant. The man who feels nothing but writes a check—he makes a difference.

There is a common misconception that great personalities such as Abraham Lincoln and Martin Luther King Jr. are remembered because of their brilliant oratory. In truth, had Lincoln not taken solid, controversial action by fighting the South to preserve the Union, and had King never marched across the South to abolish segregation, then the Gettysburg Address and the "I Have a Dream" speech would have been forgotten long ago. The reason these speeches endured was that they inspired others to take action. They inspired others to get up on their feet and protest injustice.

Actions change the world. They can also permanently alter our character. A few years ago I was walking in Jackson Square in New Orleans at around ten at night. I encountered a man holding a can wrapped in a brown paper bag. I walked over to him, took a few dollars from my wallet, and gave the bills to him. We exchanged *G-d bless you*'s. I told him not to waste the money on booze, and he assured me that he wouldn't. When I returned to join my daughter, she said, "But *Tatti*, you know he's lying! Why would you give him the money when he's just going to spend it on more beer?"

I told my daughter that I gave the man the money because for a few bucks it bought him a little dignity. And I did it for another reason. If you walk right by a guy, pretending not to even notice him, then you've dehumanized him. And dehumanized yourself by the same process. I did it for me as much as I did it for him. I want to be more sensitive to people who don't immediately engage my sympathies. Feelings follow actions because everyone wants to justify the investment they've made. A few days later my daughter copied my actions almost to the letter with a Vietnam vet she met on a street corner, because it's not a parent's words but their actions that inspire their children.

Maimonides, expanding on an old idea of Aristotle's, explained that there are two kinds of human nature. The first is our congenital nature, the character traits we possessed at birth. Modern science would call this our genetic predisposition. Some people are born passive and mild while others have a loud, competitive streak. Still others are calm until provoked, and then their fiery temper shows itself.

But the second type of human nature is not genetic but acquired. By doing the same thing over and over again, the deed becomes ingrained into our psyche. It becomes part of our personality. Its performance becomes instinctive. Habit becomes second nature. Repetitive behavior can rewrite our genetic programming and reprogram our nature. What begins as something we do ends up as something we are. *Time* magazine recently reported on the frontiers of the new science of epigenetics, and what the writer found was astounding: "Charles Darwin, whose *On the Origin of Species* celebrated its 150th anniversary in November, taught us that evolutionary changes take place over many generations and through millions of years of natural selection. But . . . scientists have now amassed historical evidence suggesting that powerful environmental conditions can somehow leave an imprint on the genetic material in eggs and sperm. These genetic imprints can short-circuit evolution and pass along new traits in a single generation." The lifestyle choices we make during our lifetimes change the ways our genes are expressed.

There's a curious verse in Exodus in which G-d says to Moses, "Go to Pharaoh, for I have hardened his heart and the hearts of his officials, so that I may perform miraculous signs of mine among them." This verse has caused confusion—don't we have free will? Maimonides explained the passage this way: Pharaoh's own habits had hardened his heart. Repetitive action becomes second nature. Pharaoh had ordered the mass extermination not of one or two people. He was not someone who murdered. Rather, he ordered that every Jewish child be drowned in the Nile. In a cold, calculated, and detached manner he committed mass murder. He was a cold-blooded killer. He had no heart. He slowly turned his heart of flesh and blood into one of stone. He had acted so dismissively of people for so long, acted spitefully and cruelly so habitually, that by the laws of nature his heart had hardened. It was impossible for him to come back. There was no humanity left in him.

To repent presupposes that there is a difference between you and the bad things you do. And repentance allows those actions to be purged from your character. But when you *become* the bad things you do, when you repeat them to the point where they become so ingrained in your character that you can no longer be purged of them, then there can be no repentance. That's what it means to have a hardened heart. Your humanity has been erased. The image of G-d that once glorified your countenance has been extinguished.

Repetitive action changes us. To return to the idea of charity for a moment: We're all born a bit selfish. Our disposition in life is toward self-preservation. For most people, the natural reaction to passing a beggar on the street is to walk right by and pretend he doesn't exist. But then, for whatever reason, a woman decides one day to smile at the guy and give him a dollar. The next day she does it again. Soon it becomes a habit. After a third and fourth time, we can predict that she'll give a dollar to a stranger when he asks. She has been changed from someone who gives charity into someone who *is* charitable. Although she began as a selfish person who occasionally practiced kindness, she is transformed into a compassionate person. If a few days go by and she hasn't run into anyone who needs help, she begins to feel uneasy. She now seeks people out.

Such is the power of action in general and repetitive action in particular. That's why it's not enough to give one or two large donations to charity per year. You're supposed to give something every day, which is why Jewish homes always have a charity box. The same is true of prayer and every other religious ritual. You're not supposed to pray when you feel like it or just when you need something. It's not supposed to be motivated only by emotion. Gratitude should not seep out of your heart only when you win the lottery. Rather, your life is supposed to become a living prayer. Jewish values are not about men and women practicing occasional hospitality, but *becoming* hospitable. In Jewish homes there are guests every Friday night rather than just at the occasional dinner party. The objective is inner transformation rather than the odd good deed.

The Christian word for helping the needy is "charity," derived from the Latin word *caritas,* or "dear." In Christianity one gives charity when one feels the plight of the poor. The downtrodden become dear to the benefactor. It is not enough to feed the poor. We must *feel* their plight. We must feel compassion. Not so in Judaism. The act of assisting the needy in Judaism, by contrast, is known as *tzedaka,* meaning "justice." When a man knocks on your door and says he is hungry, you have to feed him whether you like it or not. We couldn't care less if you feel absolutely nothing for him. You may think he's a pariah and you may insist that he smells. But who cares what you think? You have an obligation to feed him. It's an obligation of the hands, not of the heart.

Judaism concerns itself not with righteous intent but righteous action. Tzedakah means that when you earn $100, $10 of that $100 simply isn't yours. And when you give that $10 away, you're not doing anyone a favor *because it wasn't your money to begin with.* You are just the distributor. Of your income, 10 percent to 20 percent simply is not yours. You may be a temporary custodian of that money but it belongs to the poor. So you're not being nice and sweet when you give to the needy. You're acting justly.

Even if you consider a man a lazy and irresponsible parasite, you cannot withhold assistance from him. A bank manager who hates his clients still must produce their funds upon demand.

The Talmud says that "the commanded one who does a commandment is on a higher level than one who does a commandment without being commanded." This strikes most secular people as bizarre. But the reason is that in Jewish values, we don't trust the heart. A society that depends on feelings and emotions can ultimately become a very scary place. What if one day you don't feel for the poor? Should they starve? Doing anything just because you're in the mood to do it is a ruinous idea. Should a man be faithful to his wife only when they have a good sex life? What if he feels neglected or ignored? I have heard countless husbands tell me they cheated because their wives were abusive to them. Oh yeah? Well, get a divorce then. You have no right to become a liar and a cheat. You have to act justly even if you feel wronged.

Another friend of mine once lost everything in a series of bad business ventures. I went around collecting for him and his family so they could pay their mortgage and continue to live in their beautiful house. Charity is as much about dignity as it is about food and shelter—if a man suffers the humiliation of being thrown out of his own home, the chances of him recovering from his reversal of fortune and public embarrassment are slim. Then it is much more likely that he will remain dependent. One wealthy man I approached told me he would not contribute to the fund because he still saw my friend sporting Armani suits. I responded that I had not asked him for his opinion of the man in need, merely his support. Must a man don sackcloth and ashes to elicit our compassion? I didn't ask him to feel the man's pain, just to end it.

Once you start to give, your actions will drag your heart along with them, and you will end up feeling compassion as well. Likewise, sure, today the Israeli soldier is eating pork and he's got the tefillin on just to shut some kid up who was harassing him. But in a few weeks, his soul will come out and his appetite will recede.

Let's return to our husband who undertakes romantic gestures even when he's not feeling romantic. If we say that he makes those gestures to rekindle love for his wife, they are still only means to an end. Considered on those terms, loving actions are empty rituals designed to achieve our own psychic needs. So our answer to why Judaism privileges action is incomplete. If actions were important only because they led to right feelings, faith would still be the most important thing, but it's not. Showing kindness is beautiful in itself.

So back to our original question: Why is action so important? I'll start with another story. I was once counseling a couple who were having a lot of fights. The husband said his wife was insatiable. "No matter what I do," he said, "it's never enough. No matter how much affection, she still complains that she's unhappy. It's unfair. She wants too much." Then he described how she would yell at him for not thanking her for the soup she'd served for dinner. "She makes a big deal out of a bowl of soup!"

I told the husband that he didn't get it. What his wife was saying to him was "Listen to me. That is not soup. That's *love*. I am not a caterer. I'm not doing this for money or acclaim. I'm a woman, not a cook. And you're my husband and you're hungry, and so I made you some soup."

The reason action is so important is that when you truly love someone, your love is made manifest. It can extend so far that it travels all the way from your heart into a bowl of soup. But if your love is weak, it can be expressed only in more obvious ways. Some people love so powerfully, and so potently, that their love has the power to transform washing dirty dishes into an act of love. Real love can embrace and encompass even mundane action.

Other religions say that G-d is spiritual. G-d lives in the heavens. G-d doesn't marry. G-d doesn't buy things, so it cannot be that G-d can be found here in the material world. Only when they die, the thinking goes, will they rise to a spiritual realm and finally be with G-d. Jewish values ask: Why limit your experience with the divine? G-d is infinite. He is no more in the heavens than He is on earth. He extends from the highest to the lowest reaches.

Those who find G-d in actions are those who most believe in G-d's omnipresence. That's why Judaism is a religion of action. It maintains that G-d's presence is so potent that it extends into actions. G-d's love can be captured in the things we do.

Notice also that from the perspective of Jewish values, death is a curse. Bodies are buried far away from places of worship. We don't look forward to being released from our physical bodies after death. We believe G-d is found in life, and in the things that we do. He is found in actions. When Jews go to a cemetery, men are asked to tuck in their *tzitzit.* Why? By displaying your tzitzit, you are scoffing at the dead.

In other words, the dead wish they were still alive so they could perform more of G-d's commandments. So don't mock them. Their souls are in heaven, but they wish they were here, capable of actions that bind them to eternity.

I tell the single women who come to see me for counseling sessions, confused and worried about the intentions of the men they're dating, that there's a sure sign of a man's love. It is not when he's making love to her, and not when he buys her dinner. It's when he watches her carrying something and says, "Here, let me carry that for you." It's when he takes a burden off her hands. It's when he opens doors for her. When he says, "Let me do that for you." None of these actions constitute chivalry. What he is doing, rather, is demonstrating that his concern for her extends to the nitty-gritty details of everyday life.

That's what a mitzvah is—an affirmation of the truth that we can find G-d in every aspect of our lives, even in areas that appear to be mundane. We can usher Him into every arena of our existence.

Years ago an English minister wrote to me, telling me how he had worked his guts out, essentially neglecting his family, and his wife had become very lonely. When she started acting strangely, he suspected she was having an affair and he confronted her about it. She said, yes, there was someone but nothing had happened. Really, he wondered, nothing? "Well, to be honest," she continued, "I helped him for free many times with his taxes."

What an incredible statement. She wouldn't betray her marriage vows but she still wanted to *do something* for this other man. She had to connect with him through *some sort of action*.

Einstein's theory of relativity posits that all matter, ourselves included, is particles of congealed energy. "Dust are thou, and to dust shall thou return." We arise from nothingness and return to nothingness. We spring forth from the mixing together of the elements and later decompose and return to the same elements from whence we arose. The only question when we return will be how much impact we made while we were alive. Did we leave a trace?

We are not meant to grow hot and cold with the seasons, but rather to create light and warmth and brighten the earth. We are not thermometers but thermostats. The way we make a difference in the world is through the power of action. It's not what you believe that matters. *It's what you do.* Action is everything. We change ourselves and change the world not through thoughts or speeches but tangible action. It's not that thoughts and words don't matter. They do. Nike is wrong. You shouldn't "just do it." First you have to think about what is right. You have to articulate to others what is just. You have to feel a passion for what is just. And then, acting on your moral principles, you do it. But in the final analysis, action trumps motivation any day of the week.

I said motivation was inconsequential, but it can't be ignored completely. Although world redemption is our first calling, individuals should not ignore their own development as caring human beings who are sensitive to the suffering of other members of the human family. Even though the wrong motivation will not taint our good deeds, we have an obligation to improve first the macrocosm, the outer world at large, and then the microcosm, the inner world of man. Hence a complete mitzvah, or good deed, consists of the G-dly act coupled with the proper motivation.

The value of action is simple. You have to involve yourself in the world's details. You have to be nice to people when you've had a rotten day. You have to commit to a person after you've dated him or her for a couple of months. You have to put the BlackBerry down when your kids need help with homework. Never underestimate the power of one righteous action to redeem a chaotic world.

CHAPTER 5

Marriage

∞∞∞∞∞∞∞∞∞∞

Marriage may often be a stormy lake, but celibacy is almost always a muddy horse pond.
—THOMAS LOVE PEACOCK

In the opinion of the world, marriage ends all, as it does in a comedy. The truth is precisely the opposite: It begins all.
—ANNE SOPHIE SWETCHINE

L ook at the heroes of the ancient world: Julius Caesar, Hannibal, Alexander the Great. All were great conquerors, warriors lauded for their heroism, ruthlessness, and strategy. Can you name one person from antiquity who was famous for making peace? The very idea was laughable. If you refused to fight, you were a joke, a shadow of a man. But if you disemboweled someone in battle, then you might win your peers' allegiance and respect.

These great conquerors understood that the way to build a movement and preserve your borders was to hate. If you could galvanize people, if you could focus their hate and their aggression, you could build an army. With an army, you could build fortresses on land and in people's hearts.

Where did this idea that militarism was the path to greatness come from? The two most famous poems of all time are Homer's *Iliad*, about the Trojan War, and the *Odyssey*, about a journey home from war. Homer, who was a poet in Asia Minor, had contemplated the state of humankind and concluded that people's lives were pathetic. Your mother had to nurse you and you soiled your diaper. You got older and were apprenticed to a blacksmith. You plowed the fields and grew grains, and at thirty-five you dropped dead.

Homer said to himself, *That's it? This is mediocre! Boring! There must be something more.* So he invented the myth of the superhero. In giving the world his epic poems of superheroes in battle, he effectively said, *There's something I can do for you, you pathetic farmer. I can tell you stories of great men who lived lives of glory, who could leap walls and vanquish enemies. You can live vicariously through them.*

Homer's ideal man was a warrior, engaged in conquest. And the ideal woman was Helen of Troy, so stunningly beautiful that a thousand ships were launched to claim her.

This vision had two consequences. The first is that war became glorified. War was everything that everyday life wasn't—exciting, dramatic. Success in war asserted your authority and proved your manhood. The second consequence is that it made all of us feel utterly worthless. These Homeric figures were extraordinary. We were lowly farmers, but they had women whom men would risk everything for. We just had wives.

Our problem today is that the Homeric view of mankind has prevailed. We read stories in *US Weekly* and buy jerseys with Alex Rodriguez's name on the back. On Saturday nights we watch Angelina Jolie battle the bad guys. We live vicariously through celebrities and then turn on talk radio to hear hosts barking relentlessly about enemies real and imagined, because if they can stir up some heat, they get ratings that will please advertisers.

We still love combat. In sports, we look forward to the Olympics. On television, it's constant drama and hair-pulling. Football, which I confess has been my own favorite sport since I was a boy, is remarkably violent. Boxing is a sport of unequaled brutality. Now you begin to see why we've become sports fanatics and Hollywood is the most far-reaching industry on earth. Hollywood taps into our insatiable desire for conflict and heroes. Even our political coverage is largely about the horse race. Who won the battle of ideas today? Whose poll numbers are up? Which politician drove a stake through the heart of an opponent on the campaign trail? Politicians themselves are always promising to "fight" for us. They'll create change *for* us so we don't have to change ourselves. This is the deeper meaning and consequence of our militarist tendencies: We disempower ourselves.

You might be asking yourself, *What does any of this have to do with marriage? Why is marriage one of the core Jewish values? And how is marriage a value?* It's quite simple. The ancient world exalted conquerors. Then along came Jewish prophets who said there would come a time when those who looked for fights would be seen as insecure and pathetic. A time when warriors would be laughed at and the peacemakers praised. There would be a softening of human nature, leading a more nurturing generation to emerge.

The Jews also made another claim. They said a man *must* marry. Whereas in Christianity marriage is a sacrament, in Judaism it is an obligation. Jesus and St. Paul never married. But all the Jewish patriarchs had wives who shared their lives. Without their wives, in the most literal sense they would never have been patriarchs. Jewish prophecy said that raw militarism must—and would—be softened by peacemaking. So raw, masculine energy also *must* be neutralized by exposure to the feminine.

Of course, every ancient culture had a conception of the importance of uniting the feminine and masculine. In kabbalah, the union of masculine and feminine is known as *yichud zah* and *nukvah,* or *yichud zun.* The ancient Greeks believed, as Heraclites said, that "between all things there is a hidden connection, so that those that are apparently 'tending apart' are actually 'being brought together.'" The Hindu *jivanmukta,* the liberated individual, is someone who is liberated from duality and has synthesized the masculine and feminine polls into one complete package. Tantric masters strive for the union of Shiva (a Hindu god) and Shakti (his consort) in one's own body and consciousness. In Buddhist art, representation of the male deity locked in a sexual embrace with his consort illustrates the mystical union of the active force with wisdom, or *prajna,* which is feminine.

But Judaism is the only religion in which marriage is not negotiable. In Catholicism, priests and nuns—the leaders of the faith—still are forbidden to marry. The apostle Paul even thought marriage was best avoided. "I say therefore to the unmarried and widows, it is good for them if they abide even as I," he wrote to the Christian Church at Corinthians. "But if they cannot contain, let them marry: for it is better to marry than to burn." In sharp contrast, the Talmud makes a strange statement: If a man isn't married by twenty-five, G-d says *he has destroyed my world.*

What? A man who has had five girlfriends, is approaching his twenty-sixth birthday, and hasn't yet found a woman he wants to commit to, *has destroyed G-d's world?*

It sounds completely absurd. Here's what's behind that statement. If he's just a man and doesn't have a wife, then he's breathing too much aggression into the world. The hard edge of the masculine-aggressive can be ameliorated only through exposure to the feminine. Look at Wall Street's masculine, aggressive culture—the ups and downs, the premium on amassing riches and, better yet, more riches than the next guy. Notice that many Wall Street workers bring an aggressiveness even to dating. Hedge fund managers are "modelizers." They want not just a good woman but the *best* woman, the most desired woman. They introduce market values into everything. In this arena, dating is not about finding someone who meets your needs. It's about finding someone who can help you compete.

That's why dating today is so degrading. One is compared constantly. If you take love and put a price tag on it, there's nothing left to distinguish us from brutes.

The Talmud says another amazing thing about marriage: If you have found a wife, you have found good. Does it say that if you have found G-d, you have found good? No. If you have found the Torah? No. This is the only instance where something is declared an unmitigated good.

The truth is, there is no equality of the sexes. In most of the areas that define our core humanity, women have the upper hand. Men are eight times more likely to abandon their children than women are. Men are three times more likely to cheat in a relationship. Women are not porn addicts but men often are. Women go to church and synagogue twice as often as men. Women are much more prone to talk about building relationships than are men. We men need to acknowledge these gifts. We need to learn from our wives and welcome the feminine into our lives.

Evidence that men need women is everywhere. Have you ever been in an environment that was too masculine? The stench! Just the scent that hits your nose in an all-male dormitory can knock you out. Yes, I'm exaggerating, but you get the point. It's an environment that often lacks domestication. The way men live when there are no women to hold them to higher standards of graciousness and consideration can often be appalling. Men who remain bachelors for too long often go a bit "off." They become more stubborn and more set in their ways. They lack a domestic impulse. Studies even show that they are not as physically healthy as married men. They die earlier, are more prone to depression, and have much higher rates of suicide.

Imagine this: One of the most popular television shows of the past ten years was *Queer Eye for the Straight Guy*. The whole premise was that heterosexual men were so confused about masculinity, so incapable of keeping their houses and lives in order, so inept at managing their romantic relationships, that they needed the advice of not one but five gay men. In one episode, a young man was even coached in how to propose to his girlfriend.

Modern men find themselves in crisis. The most aggressive societies on the planet are those that allow no feminine input whatsoever. Hitler did not have a single woman in his leadership. We even have reports on how he treated Eva Braun—his ostensible girlfriend. In his book *Inside the Third Reich,* Albert Speer relates how Hitler would go out of his way to fool people into thinking that Braun did not exist or that she had no influence over him. Gathered with his inner circle at his Alpine retreat, he once walked over to Braun and gave her an envelope filled with cash, implying with this gesture that she was a whore. Hitler had to show that he had no softening influences in his life.

The most peacemaking societies, however, are those that welcome feminine input. Women bring nurturing energy and see through the stupidity of war and competition. They raise these soldiers and feed them; they don't want to see them die. Unlike men, they're not stupid enough to imagine that people can live without love and commitment.

At the Louvre, Nicolas Poussin's famous painting *The Rape of the Sabine Women* depicts the incident in which the Romans, having only recently founded their fledgling city, sacked the Sabines' city, stole their women, and brought the ladies back to Rome to make them their wives—a mass kidnapping. Rome was now guaranteed continuity.

But there's another painting on the subject at the Louvre. Jacques-Louis David's version depicts the Sabines coming to take revenge and their women, now married to the Romans, intervening to stop the confrontation. They didn't want their brothers killing their husbands.

What do you sometimes see happening today in Palestinian society? Instead of a mother trying to stop her fifteen-year-old from blowing himself up, she may tell him, *If you don't sacrifice your life, I'll be ashamed of you.* This is the true corruption of the feminine.

To be sure, we hope these horrific stories often reported in the media are anomalies.

Certainly in the West, we must ensure that we never do that to women. But the more women witness men's misbehavior, the more their hearts harden. *Since I'm not going to find a good man anyway,* a single woman thinks, *I'll just try to get something out of the relationship—maybe high-limit credit cards.* She becomes manipulative. What was the essence of *The Rules,* one of the biggest relationship advice books of the 1990s? Its ethos was simple and degrading: *He wants to get something out of you, namely sex, so outflank him and get him to marry you.* Men love the chase and cannot be trusted, so you women just have to outsmart him.

This is tragically close to the ideals of an ancient world, which prized masculinity and where people felt they didn't matter, that they needed to win to establish their worth.

The philosopher Hegel said that the master and slave relationship was born out of fear. Once you fear someone, and they're not afraid of you, they become your master. That's why today's twenty-four-hour cable news channels are always trying to scare the wits out of you. The more you fear, the more you will look to them for information and to tell you what to do. That's why every women's magazine is about scaring the living daylights out of you. "How to get rid of your wrinkles" is another way of saying, "You're an old bag." "How to have the greatest sex ever!" is another way of saying, "Maybe you're not good enough in bed." If you're scared, you will buy the magazine and what's advertised in it.

Our media-saturated culture thrives on competition and fear. It is very aggressive and very masculine. By Homeric standards, people in the United States should feel great—we are wealthy and powerful—and yet we're not nearly as happy as we ought to be. And sometimes we're downright miserable.

Why? We're miserable because we don't know how to stop competing. We have no warm place to call home. We don't feel comfortable in our own skin. We're constantly engaged in proving ourselves. We know how to be men. How to make money. How to get a woman into bed. But how to remain attracted to our wives for thirty years? How to raise and inspire children? We are clueless. Go to any Barnes & Noble and you'll see shelves and shelves of books on how to get married. Wasn't this once intuitive? Imagine going to the shelf and seeing *How to Breathe Properly* or *How to Eat Dinner*. Do we really need to be taught how to love?

That's why Judaism's contribution was to assert that we had to soften raw masculinity to reach our full human potential. Five hundred years ago, Rabbi Isaac Luria, the most outstanding Jewish kabbalist of all time, wrote that the Messiah would not come until husbands began to obey their wives. He was referring to the need for men to undo the damage of the sin of the golden calf—when women admonished their husbands for forgetting the G-d who had just redeemed them from Egypt. But Rabbi Luria also meant that men would have to learn that their win-lose philosophy, born of a scarcity mentality, would have to bend to the maternal, harmonious instinct of win-win, in which people support one another in an era of infinite abundance and everlasting peace.

Jewish values champion the nurturing, as opposed to the competitive, spirit within us. According to Judaism, children need to be disciplined but that need is transitory, whereas the need to be nurtured and loved is eternal. Children who are not sufficiently disciplined may still make valuable contributions to the world around them. But those who have not been loved usually are hobbled by lifelong and debilitating insecurities.

The Jewish people are the world's midwives, playing the soft woman to the harsh masculine posture of other nations. In ancient times, Gandhi and Martin Luther King Jr. would have been ridiculed. Ditto Nelson Mandela, another man who refused to fight and decided to forgive. Rather than calling for armed insurrection and wholesale slaughter of the white minority in South Africa after he had been released from prison, Mandela inspired a nation and brought warring brothers together. Later, when he assumed power, he pursued policies of reconciliation and healing. Now consider that the least respected leader from the past fifteen years is the monster Saddam Hussein. Today, saber rattlers can't get respect.

Rather, heroism is found in conquering our inner predilection toward wickedness, and bravery in acts of generosity and kindness.

Even establishment business thinking now asserts that corporate titans must think "win-win" rather than "win-lose," as Stephen Covey so forcefully argued in his best seller *The 7 Habits of Highly Effective People.* The idea of seeing one's competitor as kin and ensuring that he also benefits from a deal is a total reversal from the cutthroat commercial practices of just a generation ago.

Men who revel in their feminine energy—who are peaceful, charitable, domesticated, and loving—are respected far more than the alpha males who use bullying, fear, and intimidation to achieve their aims, because fear has a shelf-life. War does too. But love and nurturing win arguments over the long term.

Marriage is a central Jewish value because each of us could stand to be gentler. Judaism teaches us to live for Shabbat, our "bride" and queen, rather than for the masculine "days of the week," in which a man is important because of the car he drives or the titles he has earned.

I see my life as an opportunity to reverse the mistakes made by countless men of earlier generations who, with the best of intentions, put their careers before their families. Before I am accused of hypocrisy, let me readily admit that I am still far from that goal. But women have the power to bring redemption to men. The main lesson a wife can teach her husband is to be satisfied with her love and that of their children, rather than needing the adulation of the crowd. Wives who push their husbands to ever-higher planes of professional achievement are doing them a disservice. If not women, who will correct errant men who sacrifice all that is good in their lives?

Maimonides said that people are naturally extremists. In fact, you are more likely to bump into an extremist on the streets than a fully balanced person. Marriage forces us to find balance. In so doing, we move the world closer to redemption.

CHAPTER 6

Struggle

∞∞∞∞∞∞∞∞∞∞∞

There are no classes in life for beginners; right away you are always asked to deal with what is most difficult.

—RAINER MARIA RILKE

Only mediocrity can be trusted to be always at its best.

—MAX BEERBOHM

Life can bend people out of shape. They reach middle age and find themselves cynical, dejected, broken. Life's problems have literally misshapen their bodies. They are overweight or underweight. Disappointment and anger have also misshapen their minds. They are no longer open and curious, but fearful and confused. Their hearts have shriveled and shrunk—sometimes sutured shut altogether.

Suffering can shadow an entire nation's history. One Sunday afternoon a young Oxford student in a rush came to see me, saying that the school chaplain had told him that if his mother was Jewish, he was a Jew, even if his father wasn't. The student asked me whether this was correct, and I said it was. He said, "But I don't want to be Jewish." He said he'd researched his options and found out that I could excommunicate him. Would I please do so?

I wasn't thrilled about this but he was very persistent. So to make a point, I typed out a phony certificate for him. As he snatched that worthless piece of paper out of my hands and began to rush back out the door, I asked him why he didn't want to be Jewish. He was a history major, he said, and he had studied how the Greeks philosophized, how the Romans conquered, how the British sailed, how the Americans built fortunes— and how the Jews died. Century after century, it was always how the Jews died, and he didn't want any part of this legacy.

But he neglected something, I told him. To discover a Roman or a Spartan, he had to open a history book. But to find a Jew, he just had to walk into my office. For all his complaints that the Jews have been so hated and so weak, we're still around, and the mightiest empires have crumbled. The Jews are masters at taking darkness and turning it into light, at taking death and turning it into life, at taking suffering and turning it into a blessing, at taking our flaws and turning them into courage and heroism. Where most of the world believes in perfection, Jews believe in struggle.

The Jewish Bible has not a single perfect person. The Torah is very specific about Abraham's flaws, portraying him in a somewhat negative light when he tells Sarah, "Look, tell Pharaoh that I'm your brother." Later, he is forced to choose between Sarah and his son Ishmael, whom he has failed to raise properly, and he sends Ishmael away. Isaac has Esau, a charlatan who later seeks to kill his own brother. Jacob's kids? That's a pretty dysfunctional family. Jacob loves his son Joseph so much that his other sons conspire to kill Joseph. As for Moses, the greatest prophet of all time, his sin is taken so seriously by G-d that he can't even enter the land of Israel. Moses also fails to turn the heart of the people to focus permanently on G-d. What about the Jewish people who wander the desert for forty years? G-d is so fed up with them a few times that he wants to destroy them! As for King David, he is so riddled with flaws that he must live through the open rebellion of his beloved Absalom.

So if these people were so flawed, why do we still read about them? Why are they the great leaders of the nation? And why do we seek to emulate their example?

Simple. These men and women were great because they struggled to do right amid a predilection to do otherwise.

The reason there are no perfect people in the Torah is that we don't believe in perfect people and we do not respect perfection. Do you know what the perfect person lacks that the imperfect person has? An imperfect person fights to do what is right. He struggles with his conscience. When you fight for something, you demonstrate its worth.

Look at the contrast with every other belief system. Christianity is predicated on perfection, on the idea that Jesus was tempted but never fell. The same is true for Muslims and Mohammed. In Buddhism, the Buddha is perfect. In Hinduism, Krishna is perfect. Even in the pantheon of great American heroes, our founding fathers were once portrayed as saints. I remember being taught as a young boy that George Washington never told a lie and that Abraham Lincoln walked miles to return a single penny. Both these stories were pure invention, but the idea was: How could you respect the founder of your nation if he was flawed?

Here in America we live under the tyranny of perfection. We are constantly being sold glossy images of people with perfect bodies, perfect résumés, and perfect lifestyles. Convincing people of their inadequacy in relation to these paragons of physical, intellectual, moral, and aesthetic perfection has always been a good racket, but never more so than today.

It even seeps into our religious debates. The insinuation that Jesus was lonely and required the love of a woman, as Dan Brown suggested in *The Da Vinci Code,* deeply offended many of our Christian brothers and sisters. When I debated Cardinal Theodore McCarrick of Washington, D.C., about the subsequent movie, he said that the film's protestors should remain calm but he could understand why people were upset. I said I understood how the departure from New Testament orthodoxy was provocative, but why was it deemed so *hurtful*? Dan Brown and the moviemakers didn't say anything bad about Jesus—they said only that he got married! So what? If he were a young Jewish man growing up in the Galilee region in ancient Israel, not only would he have been expected to marry but *it would have been sinful for him not to.*

Why were Christians offended at the thought that Jesus married? Because the idea suggests he felt something was missing in his life. In short, he wasn't perfect. As a perfect being, he required the love and validation of no one. You and I? We get cold and need comfort and want to be held. We feel dispirited, and we need someone to inspire us.

I am always impressed at the deep spirituality of my Christian brothers. I am a rabbi with a deep love and awe for the incredible commitment to goodness and faith that is so characteristic of my Christian colleagues. But ultimately Christianity loses me when it dismisses the humanity of Jesus in favor of his divinity. Jesus is so much more interesting when we read of his struggles in the New Testament to fulfill the will of G-d, like when he says, while dying on the cross, "My G-d, my G-d, why have you forsaken me?" And I am always puzzled why my Christian brothers and sisters seem disheartened to discover Jesus's vulnerabilities.

Personally, I have no patience for perfect people. I find them boring, predictable, and judgmental. It is human beings whose goodness is real, yet purchased amid Herculean effort and struggle, whom I find so endlessly fascinating.

Judaism doesn't value perfection. I believe that perfect people are sweet and nice but I have no relationship with them, nor would I seek one. If they're perfect, they don't need me. It has been estimated that in many marriages, the criticism-to-compliment ratio is three to one. The argument troubled couples make is always essentially, "but my spouse is so imperfect!" I counsel them to remember that if their spouse were perfect, he or she would never have married in the first place. So why not be thankful for our loved ones' imperfections (as long as they take responsibility for their actions and apologize sincerely when they've done wrong)?

I am not a Christian not because I was born Jewish, because if Christianity were my personal truth I would be obligated to convert. Rather, the attainment of perfection has no appeal for me. Perfect people do the right thing every single time. How could they understand someone like me, for whom every day is a struggle?

Being with perfect people is like watching a movie when you already know the ending. You can't thrill to perfect people's victories because they don't involve real courage. Real courage means to be victorious over fear. If you were never afraid, were your actions courageous? No.

People used to think Martin Luther King Jr. was a saint. He started the civil rights movement when he was only twenty-four years old. He was killed before his fortieth birthday. Of course, one thought, saint that King was, he was able to lead those marches in Birmingham and in Selma and inspire a whole generation. No wonder he was so incredibly eloquent and courageous. He was perfect. But then we discovered that in fact he was deeply human and did things that betrayed big character flaws. Suddenly we saw him differently. In fact, his true greatness was thereby manifest: He was flawed and frail and *still* he accomplished so much. You mean he was *scared* in front of those attack dogs and Bull Connor? He had to struggle to do those things? My G-d, that truly is a great man.

To me, that is so much more inspiring. King wrestled with his conscience. *Now* he speaks to me, because I'm just like him. He was not an angel, not a saint, just a person who struggled to live righteously and courageously. King, while of course a Christian, constantly quoted the prophets of the Hebrew Bible. And I believe that it was their example that propelled him to engage in the struggle for racial equality and justice. As he so often said, "Let justice roll like a river and righteousness like a mighty spring" (Amos 5:24). And in so doing he changed America, dealt a fatal blow to racial injustice, and restored the country to its founding creed of all men being created equally by G-d. And he did all this not intuitively or instinctively, but amid great effort and struggle. It was never easy. But if he could do it and he was human like me, then I have no excuse not to try to rise to similar acts of courage.

The truly righteous man is not he who never sins but rather he who, amid a predilection to narcissism and selfishness, battles his nature to live a virtuous life. The truly great man is not he who slays dragons, but he who battles his inner demons, who struggles with himself to improve and ennoble his character.

The truth is that perfection fosters dependency. It is an engine that actually retards human progress, because it continually tosses humans back on a sense of their own inadequacy. Rather than lift them up, it keeps them down. That's why kings used to claim they were perfect beings, kissed by G-d and standing high above their lowly subjects—because if you can convince people that they'll never be as good as you, they won't even try. They will worship you and hate themselves.

A mature understanding of the value of struggle, however, is incredibly empowering. My friend Cory Booker once told me how when he was a little boy, he idolized his father. He thought his father was Superman and Mister Rogers rolled into one. Then one day his father lied to him about something. When Cory discovered the lie, he was heartbroken and his whole image of his father was turned on its head. But then after he thought it through, he learned to respect his father even more, because now he knew his father was not perfect, and yet still was such an amazing man. All the good his father had done had not come easily but rather had come about through struggle.

Those for whom life has been so sweet and smooth, those who refuse to struggle, will never know the true taste of courage. They will never develop the ability to overcome obstacles to do what is right. They will never firmly establish that their convictions are not just feelings. Struggle is where the infinite value of goodness is established.

The Zohar says that every single time you choose to subdue and subjugate evil, G-d's glory rises higher and higher. Every time you exert the effort to choose righteousness over selfishness, you are showing that righteousness is precious to you, that G-d is a living presence, and that you are prepared to fight. Even when it's inconvenient. Even when it entails sacrifice. Struggle is what establishes the infinite preciousness of righteousness.

Israel literally means "he who wrestles with G-d." It was the name given to Jacob, who wrestled with a brother who sought to kill him and a father-in-law who sought to enslave him. Most of all, he wrestled with an angel. Israel is he who wrestles with the G-dly portion of his existence.

Most of what we cherish in life involves a struggle. I was a child of divorce, so I was extremely excited to be married. I anticipated perfection. Shortly after our wedding in Australia, I went out, a newly married man, to buy a camera. And in the camera store I couldn't help but notice that the woman behind the counter was pretty. I was mortified. *This is ridiculous!* I thought. *What kind of husband am I?* I came home and confessed to my wife that I had noticed that another woman was attractive. She laughed at my naïveté. But it still bothered me, so I thought deeply into this. Why did G-d make love so imperfect? How do we even notice the opposite sex when we are in love with our spouse? Why is it that even in the best marriages we still recognize that other people are special?

Now I understand why G-d made love imperfect. Relationships are special when you choose each other anew every single day. Some think marriage is when you choose your spouse under the chuppah—the canopy used in Jewish weddings—and you're done. Married! You never make that choice again, and your choice becomes a thing of the past. The marriage becomes stale and ossified, and the commitment is never renewed. But because we all struggle to keep the passion and intimacy in our marriages alive, because we struggle to compliment and love each other, because we wrestle with our nature to always focus on each other, love each other, and put each other first, we choose each other over and over again, and that's why love is imperfect. The man who chooses his bride and never has to choose her again is one who takes her for granted, who doesn't seek to bring novelty to his relationship, who allows it to stagnate. But if you forever renew your commitment and investment, your goodness and your relationship never go stale.

"WWJD?" is a famous mantra here in America. Should I gossip about my friends? Buy a Hummer? You're supposed to ask the question, "What would Jesus do?" I am happy that it works for some people. But it doesn't work for me. The deified Jesus doesn't speak to me. What can he possibly understand about my struggle? He tells me to give away a large percentage of my income to charity when I am struggling to cover my own bills? And yes, I get it. Ten percent of what I earn is not mine. But that feels pretty darn theoretical to me, since I'm the one who worked for it and earned it. And it's a struggle for me to accept that I am its custodian to give it to those in need. How could he possibly know how difficult that is? He wasn't selfish and had no needs! WWJD? Well, we've settled that—he would always do the right thing! But what does that have to do with me? Nothing.

What would Abraham do? He would fall, pick himself up, and try again. What would David do? He would probably push his luck. Then, after his transgression, he would allow a prophet to come to him and say, *I don't care if you're the king, you have acted with great injustice.* Would David then have this challenge to his authority and reputation killed? No, he would sit down in sackcloth and ashes and compose one of the most moving psalms, Psalm 51. In that moment of mourning and regret, he would reveal a completely different facet of his nature. He would prostrate himself before G-d. "Have mercy on me, O G-d. For I know my transgressions, and my sin is always before me. . . . Do not cast me from your presence or take your Holy Spirit from me."

We have all done things for which we are ashamed. And we have all heard the voice of conscience that calls us back. We have all struggled and wrestled to heed that voice instead of simply quashing it.

Evolutionary psychology tells us that it's unnatural for men to be faithful to their wives. And so today's world is one of paralyzing extremes. Our dominant religions tell us that we must strive for perfection. On the other extreme, we're told by these same religions that we are so flawed that we can't do anything about it. Standing in the middle is the Jew, who wrestles with his inner demons. He fights his selfish nature to be a loving and good man. The Jewish values proclaim that righteousness is not instinctual and is never effortless. It is an act of courage and it leads to greatness.

The Lubavitcher Rebbe was a Jewish giant of the twentieth century. I was there watching as a millionaire gave him a new Cadillac to replace his old jalopy Cadillac. The Rebbe asked, "What's this?" "It's a present," the donor said. The Rebbe's immediate words were from Proverbs: "He who hates presents will live." It was very cold outside, and a small crowd had gathered, imploring him to get into the new car.

He refused: "Where's the old car?" And the people said, "Please, Rebbe, take the car." "No. Where's the other car?" It took fifteen minutes to track the old jalopy down. The new Cadillac was given to one of the Rebbe's secretaries.

This moment still inspires me. That a man can resist what I often live for: recognition, respect, nice things, fancy clothes. That you can be that famous and that humble.

We have to look at our everyday struggles in a different light. We have to stop letting life get us down. We have to stop feeling defeated. We have to stop being depressed and dejected. We can instead see the struggles we face each day as challenges that establish our uniqueness.

I would personally choose the man who has wrestled and struggled any day over the trust-fund kid who has never struggled. Those who have been given too many gifts often lack empathy and risk becoming conventional and one-dimensional.

But the ability to continue along the right path and be hated—that's what struggle is all about.

Jews have suffered murder and hatred throughout history, and there was always some justification for the hatred. *They really did charge a lot of interest,* people will say. *They claimed to be the chosen people, and so naturally that annoyed other nations.* Not only are we the most hated nation, we also are seen as responsible for the crimes committed against us.

So why not just assimilate? That's what some argued before the creation of Israel—that the secret to undoing anti-Semitism was to become Christian. Here's the answer: You do right because it's right when there is no reward for it. When you end up being tortured and gassed for it. When no good deed goes unpunished, you still do the right thing. You engage in the struggle.

Indeed, the ancient rabbis contrast Abraham, who defended the wicked inhabitants of Sodom and Gomorrah, with Noah, who is informed by G-d of the destruction of all mankind yet offers no protest whatsoever. This, they maintain, is the reason Abraham rather than Noah fathered the chosen people.

One final thought on the real-world implications of embracing the value of struggle: If you look at the really great men and women in history, they were always hated in their time for doing the right thing. No president was more hated than Abraham Lincoln. People in the North hated him maybe even more than those in the South. He struggled to be re-elected and was ultimately assassinated. Winston Churchill was the most hated British statesman of the 1930s. Before WWII, the British public wanted to believe Neville Chamberlain that Hitler posed no direct threat. Then moments after the Allies secured victory, and Hitler was defeated, Churchill was voted out of office.

It's nice to be loved. It's nice to go to heaven. But those who struggle for righteousness will never win popularity contests. At his son's bar mitzvah, a father tries hard to find the one message his son will take with him for the rest of his life. Not long ago, I told my son he should never do anything just to be popular. Never do anything to get applause. The only true joy we humans ever know comes from doing the right thing. It is the joy that comes from having the courage of your convictions. The joy of knowing that you may have regrets, but that you're not two people. You are whole. You're a child of G-d. And no matter how many flaws you have, you will still do your utmost to live with righteousness.

CHAPTER 7

Sacred Time

∞∞∞∞∞∞∞∞∞∞

*If once a man indulges himself in murder, very
soon he comes to think little of robbing; and from
robbing he next comes to drinking and Sabbath-
breaking, and from that to incivility and
procrastination.*

—THOMAS DE QUINCEY

*One who celebrates Shabbat will be given an
inheritance without, indeed beyond, limitation.*

—TALMUD, SHABBAT 118A

My friend Marianne Williamson has diagnosed the problem perfectly: We live in a culture of meaningless distraction. We are addicted to distraction and we don't even realize it. CNN reported in
December 2009 that the average person watches nearly five hours of TV
per day. That is a lot of time. And what are they watching? C-list celebrities
eating tarantulas on reality shows? Round-the-clock news and opinion-
mongering? What a waste. Then you have kids who fritter away their

time with video games, YouTube, and endless texting. But when you think about it, our lives are nothing but a span of time. So why aren't we more conscious of using our time, which is nothing less than our very life, more wisely?

And why are we drawn to junk as a distraction? In February 2000 Fox ushered in the age of reality TV with *Who Wants to Marry a Multi-Millionaire?* Ever since, we have lived in a world where people so desire to escape their own reality that they will escape to someone else's. We have also developed a voracious appetite for fame and to live vicariously through Hollywood glamour and celebrity train wrecks. Every year Hollywood breaks all previous box office records as people see paying ten bucks as the ultimate bargain to flee reality. But mostly we distract ourselves by shopping until we drop, using consumption as the ultimate escape from unsatisfying lives.

These escapes have only made our problems worse. After 9/11 we delegated the fight against terrorism to a warrior class of just 2 percent of the population and refused to even watch their dead bodies come home for burial, busy as we were watching *Dancing with the Stars*. We then refused to even pay for our wars and just added it on to a national debt that at the end of the decade reached the staggering sum of $12 trillion. Having not been content to nearly destroy our economy through truly reckless government and personal spending binges, we added one further escape—in the form of Internet porn, which has grown, by some reports, to occupy an hour a day for tens of millions of men.

In the meantime, as we directed our time away from the meaningful to the truly meaningless and even destructive, our relationships suffered. Singles became the majority population for the first time in American history. And as we escaped, we scarcely asked ourselves what we were escaping from. What was so uninviting about our lives that we were constantly running from them? What was inadequate about our marriages that we spent much of the decade discussing Brad and Angelina's non-marriage? What was so boring about our kids that we obsessed over

Madonna's adopted kids? And what gaping hole opened inside us that re-quired shoving an endless number of electronics, cars, and jewelry into it?

The principal reason for our escape is the absence of G-dly meaning in our lives. The material plenitude of the '80s and '90s brought about a gradual spiritual corrosion. We began to lust for objects rather than pur-pose. We allowed a career to take the place of a calling. Friends came to supplant family. Relationships based on common interests replaced com-mitments based on common purpose.

In the process we allowed shallowness and laziness to creep into our souls. Through it all we lost an appreciation for the sublimity of time. Of the two components of our world, time and space, people value the latter over the former. They will work their fingers to the bone or sit staring at a computer screen for hours to acquire property, or space. Four years to get a college degree. Ten hours per day to get a paycheck. In short, time is seen as a means to getting something else. Time is seen as valuable only insofar as it can be used to acquire things we want.

To say that this approach has shortcomings is putting the matter most mildly. Love is built not by possessions but by time. Not even quality time, but quantity time. There are no shortcuts to spending time with your kids. You can use every excuse in the book, but if you don't take the time to read to them when they're young, have dinner with them every night as they grow up, and guide them as young adults, you will never have a satisfying relationship with them. But what many parents do is extend the space-is-more-important-than-time principle to parenting. To com-pensate for the lack of time spent, they buy their children things. Only it doesn't work—and it never will.

Jewish values exalt not space but sacred time. Objects are always sub-ordinate to precious moments. Rather than use time to acquire property, we do the opposite. The purpose of having money is to facilitate special times and memorable moments. A mother works hard and uses her money to fly her kids home from college for Thanksgiving. A husband exerts himself on the job not so he can come home and commune with the couch, but so he can spend a relaxing evening with his wife, calm in the knowledge that they're not going to be sitting in darkness because the electricity has been shut off.

Space facilitates time. Those who master that idea end up having great relationships and a blessed life. But those who make the mistake of thinking that the only purpose time serves is to acquire money end up shallow and lonely materialists.

Humans are meant to expend space while acquiring time. "Remember the days of old, consider the years long past." The Bible exhorts us to embrace time as life's most precious gift. That's why the Sabbath is Judaism's holiest component. It's designed around the idea that man should work six days so he can enjoy a tranquil and uninterrupted period of intimate time with G-d and loved ones. Jewish values emphasize sacred time because we're supposed to take the ordinary and make it extraordinary. We're capable of taking moments that would have been fleeting and instead meeting G-d in them as a living presence.

For the majority of history, Jews have not been on their own land and have not had a temple. The Holy Land, the Land of Israel, is a tiny place the length and breadth of which can be driven in a few hours. But the process of hallowing time is endless. The very first act of consecration recorded in the Bible is when G-d hallowed the Sabbath day. The first time the word "holy" appears in the Bible is Genesis 2:3, in connection with the Sabbath day: "So G-d blessed the seventh day and made it holy, because on it G-d rested from all the work that he had done in creation." The first commandment given to the Jewish people when they came out of Egypt was to witness the monthly rebirth of the moon and declare the day Rosh Chodesh, the first day of the new month.

Judaism is the only religion in which time sanctifies space. To be sure, there are some beautiful synagogues and there were, of course, the two great temples in Jerusalem, the first destroyed by the Babylonians and the second by the Romans. Mount Moriah, where the temple was built in Jerusalem, was sacred because according to tradition, it was there that

G-d took clay from the earth, fashioned it into the guise of a man, breathed life into it, and called that person Adam. On the same site, many centuries later, Abraham was commanded to bring his son Isaac as a sacrifice to G-d and ended up substituting a ram in his place. Special moments and supernatural events lend a location its solemnity and sanctity—not the other way around.

In other religions, space consecrates time. Any traveler through Christian Europe will see the great monuments to space that the believers of old built for their Lord. Wondrous cathedrals of unmatched splendor rise toward the heavens. Spires carved of marble and granite scrape the sky. To go to a holy place, you may have to undertake a long and arduous journey, leaving behind home and family, as many pilgrims have discovered.

But to enter into a holy time, you need only remain in your natural surroundings and the sacred moment will catch up and overtake you, like a boat rising in the high tide.

G-d made many wondrous things but none so special as the Sabbath. The Sabbath brings rest and refreshment to a toiling planet. The concept of a day of family and community, sanctified by G-d Himself, is one of the greatest spiritual and social contributions Judaism has made to the rest of the world. It is a time in which we undergo an "attitudinal chiropractic readjustment," as Marianne Williamson put it at one of our "This World" values seminars. It is a time in which the distractions that masquerade as necessities are off-limits, and in drawing close to G-d, our relationships and we are healed.

In our family, the happiest time is Friday night and Saturday day. I even launched a national program called "Turn Friday Night into Family Night," where huge numbers of families of every persuasion have signed up to be part of what we call the "triple two." Every Friday night around dinnertime, you give yourself and your family two hours free of phone calls, BlackBerrys, and TV. Then, to teach your children the art of hospitality, you invite two guests. Finally, you prepare two substantive subjects—which we often suggest on our Web site—to raise the family discourse to something more than the latest film. Presto. You have transformed what would have been a regular TV night into the Holy Sabbath.

And what a blessing it is. In fact, the idea for "This World: The Values Network" came to me while walking with my wife one Saturday afternoon. I was explaining to her that for all my satisfaction in writing books and broadcasting, I still felt like a cowboy, an isolated voice, when it came to spreading values. Since no one person could do what a group could do, I wanted to create an organization that would mint others in spreading these special values. And so an idea was born. Had it been a Thursday, I would have been at my desk rather than walking with my wife. Even if we had been on a Thursday night walk, I would not have been focusing on spiritual self-evaluation. Only when we're unencumbered by material concerns can we really focus on the purpose and direction of our lives.

The creative pause, devoted to spiritual renewal and family connection, was utterly unknown in the ancient world. In fact, the Jews suffered ridicule on account of it from some of Rome's most prolific literary figures, including Seneca, Juvenal, and Tacitus. They thought the Jews were lazy. Why did they take off one day a week? But the biblical, seven-day week now prevails in every culture and civilization on earth.

All attempts to change this pattern and move the day of rest into a different time frame—including establishing a ten-day week during the French Revolution to accommodate a more rational decimal system— have met with failure.

As with most radical ideas, however, it has been watered down and its power diffused. Our business-oriented world treats rest as something we do just so we can keep working. Of course, workers will be more productive if they have to reinvigorate themselves. But is that really the point? Did G-d provide the Sabbath so that man might labor harder the other six days? This shallow utilitarian understanding of the Sabbath perpetuates the mistake I discussed above, namely, the subordination of time to space. Leon Trotsky said he would preserve the Sabbath, even in the atheistic culture of the Soviet Union, because all workers needed time off.

This rationale stems from the idea that our noblest goal is work rather than moments of connection and spiritual reflection.

Many people make the mistake of thinking that the prohibition against working on the Sabbath (Exodus 20:10) means that as long as they don't go to their jobs on Saturday, they are not desecrating the Sabbath. That's not enough. Sacred time also means *passive* time.

Let me explain. The frenetic activity of modern life, where things are always beeping, buzzing, and vibrating, prevents us from indulging the passive side of our nature. Obsessed as we are with doing, we rarely simple *are*. The passive state makes us anxious and uncomfortable. We get antsy and want to "go do something." Even in everyday conversation, we find it difficult to merely listen. Instead, we bob our heads to show that we are listening, or we interrupt. We feel uncomfortable when people give us compliments, because we don't know how to receive them. Many people find the passive state massively disconcerting.

It's even disconcerting for many religious people. In a public debate I participated in, a leading Reform rabbi said it was ludicrous that in the modern age we should continue to ban such activities as lighting a fire or driving on the Sabbath. He argued that the Sabbath was a day of rest, and therefore anything a person found restful, such as gardening or going to a concert or football game, would be consistent with the spirit of the day. He promoted the idea that lighting a fire on the Sabbath was once prohibited because of the labor involved—rubbing stones and sticks together to generate a spark.

But the Sabbath is not just a day of rest from work. The Sabbath is a day where we rest from *creativity*, from trying to make an impact on the world. Instead we learn to be part of our environment. We learn just to be. The theme of the Sabbath is that G-d created heaven and the earth in six days. On the seventh day He rested and commanded us to do the same. So on the Sabbath we rest from the kind of work G-d undertook in the original six days, creative labor. We don't try to improve ourselves relative to our environment. Rather, we become one with the universe.

The Sabbath day was given for humans to acknowledge their role as components of creation, not masters of it.

Ever see someone who can't keep still? She'll be sitting quietly at a café table, and yet underneath, she frantically taps her right foot? The Yiddish language has a word for this—*shpilkes,* an excess of nervous energy. The kabbalah offers an interesting take on it: Divine illumination comes to you, but if you're not prepared to receive the revelation, it's like pouring too much water into a fragile vase. The vase shatters. Similarly, if we don't prepare ourselves to receive the light of the universe through the ritual and restoration of the Sabbath, our nervous system shatters. The Sabbath thus offers a cure for anxiety.

The Sabbath is also a remedy for arrogance. From the beginning of time, humans have been engaged in a constant battle against nature. By exercising our intelligence, and through hard work, we bring nature to heel and subjugate it to our dominion. We erect buildings and raise capital. Our ability to control disease and prevent floods testifies to the huge progress we've made in slowly mastering nature. But a danger looms over us as a result of our success, and that's the possibility—nay, the likelihood—that we will forget that we too are creatures and that G-d is the ultimate master. Many people wonder how Germany, the most cultured nation on earth, the nation that produced the greatest philosophers and scientists throughout the 1920s, could have become so savage just a few years later. The answer is that it was precisely the mastery of so many disciplines that made the country's leaders think they could master life and death as well. Whenever people forget their limitations, they become downright scary. Yes, we humans are endowed with extraordinary creativity. But that can easily lead to self-deification.

In the same way that people are distinguished by their intelligence, labor, and art, these attributes can lead humans to make idols of their own selves. Think of an NBA star who begins to believe his own press. His life becomes an endless cycle of sexual conquests, and women exist solely to satisfy his needs. Or the dictator who has so much power that he begins to think he owns his people as well. Or the woman for whom shopping is the week's greatest thrill, or the man and woman who delay marriage well into their forties, busy as they are climbing the corporate ladder. Too much work can turn us all into shallow, even dangerous monoliths.

We can all be grateful for the enormous technological advances of the past century, but perhaps we are beginning to create too much. Like Dr. Frankenstein, is there not a danger that we can cross a line that can lead to catastrophe? The creative side of humanity is always in danger of being deified. Not long ago, art focused on religious subjects. Now religion is not intrinsically a better subject than any other in art, but the fact does demonstrate that mankind once felt obligated to devote creative energy to praising higher pursuits. In 1993, when terrorists exploded a car bomb outside the Uffizi Gallery in Florence, the newspapers first gave a detailed report on which masterpieces had been damaged. Only later did they mention that people had died in the blast as well. Such idolization of human craftsmanship is precisely what the Sabbath is designed to combat.

By refraining from creative labor for one day a week, and dedicating that day to G-d, we acknowledge G-d's mastery over the earth and our dependency upon Him for life and sustenance. By refraining from creating, we learn our true place as part of, rather than masters of, creation. That is why even recreational activities such as gardening or playing music, in which we take elements of G-d's universe and use our own creative talents to try to improve them, are off-limits. Generally speaking, the labors prohibited on the Sabbath are as follows: any constructive activity that makes some significant, useful change in our material environment. Some of the more common prohibitions for the Sabbath include plowing, sowing, reaping, baking, bleaching, dyeing, tying a knot, tearing, trapping or hunting, building, demolishing, kindling a fire, writing, erasing, sewing, grinding, cooking, and putting the finishing touches on a newly manufactured article. Thousands of tributary forms of work are prohibited within the thirty-nine main categories. One example is turning on any form of electrical appliance, because it completes, or builds, a circuit, allowing the free flow of electrons; thus it constitutes both building and completing a manufactured article.

Carrying something from a private to a public domain, say, from your house into the street, is also prohibited. Desisting from carrying acknowledges G-d's sovereignty over all affairs of society. Carrying from place to place signifies commerce and the exchange of ideas and goods between people in society. Transferring material objects from one domain to another is characteristic of work by which humans pursue their purposes in business and elsewhere. It is an a priori expression of ownership and dominance and is therefore prohibited on the Sabbath, a day on which the earth and its host are consecrated to a more exalted proprietor. A community that ceases carrying on the Sabbath acknowledges G-d as its master and puts the seal of divine approval on all its programs and aspirations.

For six days of every week, we humans use our own contributions to enhance the raw materials the Almighty created. We cut down trees and build houses, cook raw vegetables and make them edible, and cure diseases with medicines. In so doing, humans are living up to their highest human calling, to imitate G-d Himself. Just as G-d is a creator, so too is man. Humans are welcomed, even obligated, to join G-d as a junior partner in creation. But one day a week, the world is elevated to a higher state of perfection. On that day, we see the world differently. It doesn't need tinkering or improving. It just needs to be left alone.

Relationships also need to be left alone at times—another lesson of the Sabbath. I spend much of the week raising my kids, by which I mean that I lecture them to do their homework, make sure they tidy their rooms, and order them to clean up after dinner. But on the Sabbath I just enjoy them. I am not there to shape and mold them that day. They need no "raising." That one day, they are perfect just the way they are. And imagine how corrosive our relationship might become if I never stopped lecturing them and ordering them around.

Consider this: How did we come to destroy the environment? Simple. We saw the earth as something that could withstand endless tinkering. We saw trees and thought they would make useful furniture. We took a look at rivers and saw in them a giant toilet for factory waste. And we peered at elephants and saw great sources of ivory. In each of these cases, the human sin involved seeing the world as a means rather than as an end. We robbed the world of its awe, majesty, and wonder. We made it ordinary, reducing it to utilitarian ends. Without a Sabbath we risk doing the same thing with our kids. Rather than seeing a beautiful child, we see someone who can do better on his SATs and get into Harvard. After a while the child begins to feel like a circus monkey trained to get good grades and impress his teachers and parents.

The Sabbath is not about learning a sense of priorities, the relative values of urgency and importance. The beauty of the Sabbath is that on this day there simply is *nothing urgent*. The Talmud explains that at the completion of the six days the world was missing one pivotal ingredient: peace. "When the Sabbath came, peace came with it." The serenity of the Sabbath—an island of calm in the turbulent seas of commercialization—offers an environment of tranquility and quiet.

The Sabbath is a great equalizer. The Bible commands that on the Sabbath day the bondsman and the maidservant must rest, just as their master rests. Imagine how revolutionary a teaching this was in earlier times, when servants were seen as nothing more than the animated tools of their masters. By recurring weekly, the Sabbath reminds us that every human being possesses an intrinsic and infinite worth that cannot be measured in commercial terms. Without the Sabbath, we ourselves become servants.

The Sabbath liberates us from the pressure to skew our priorities. My old dentist is an Orthodox Jew and a close friend. Although a consummate professional, on one occasion he put a filling in my tooth that cracked. I could not eat on that side of my mouth and called him at home, telling his daughter that it was urgent. She returned to the phone saying her father was busy. "Tell him it's an emergency," I said. "My filling has broken." She again returned to the phone. "My daddy said he is celebrating his mother's eighty-second birthday, and you will just have to call him in the morning at the office." The Bible says that honoring one's parents is a sacred duty. Here was a man who treated his mother as the Sabbath. My tooth would have to wait.

The Bible does not require that humans be idle on the Sabbath—indeed, the Torah sees inactivity as harmful, and a misuse of leisure as deleterious to our mental health. What the Bible seeks is to invert our creative talents, where the focus is not on perfection of the external world of the senses but perfection of the internal world of the spirit. One day of the week, men and women focus on internal perfection as the goal of their creative capacity.

Modern men and women have lost a sense of their own uniqueness. They define themselves almost entirely by their productive output. But rest, rather than work, leads to self-discovery. Whereas through work we attempt to master creation by using our creative talents, through rest we learn to master ourselves, a far greater challenge. Throughout the week we attempt to master the world around us. On the Sabbath we attempt to conquer the world inside us.

Paradoxically, this does not require a sacrifice in the material world, the one in which we work hard to get ahead. The realignment the Sabbath offers us will be seen and noticed and felt by the people we encounter. How is this possible? It's because people meet us at the level at which we speak. If we speak foolishly, they'll connect to us as fools. If we're panicked and anxious, people will feel panicked and anxious around us. But if we are infused with G-d's light, if we have access to a deep, divine peace, people will recognize the G-dly within us. This doesn't mean they'll do whatever we say or want! But we become impossible to ignore.

We pay a terrible price in the world for not giving time to G-d. If we aren't close to G-d, if we don't have an integrated sense of who we are as children of G-d, then we occupy a frazzled, fractured space. Our conversations will suffer. We'll talk for hours but no one will take us seriously. Our friendships and our working relationships will diminish in quality. People will look at us and not see blinding light but instead shades of gray. They will see someone living a truly compromised life. Monday through Friday we move away from G-d and from our truest selves. On the Sabbath we return to G-d and to our selves. Whenever human dignity is assaulted by distractions and threatened by purposelessness, sacred time comes to our rescue.

CHAPTER 8

Gratitude

∞∞∞∞∞∞∞∞∞∞

*Gratitude is not only the greatest of virtues, but
the parent of all the others.*

—CICERO

*To educate yourself for the feeling of gratitude
means to take nothing for granted, but to always
seek out and value the kindness that stands
behind the action. Nothing that is done for you is
a matter of course.*

—ALBERT SCHWEITZER

Gratitude is one of the most central of all values, and some would
say it's the most important. He who does not feel gratitude has,
for all intents and purposes, compromised his humanity. Those who feel
no gratitude remain untouched by the kindnesses performed for them.
Their spirits are not moved. In the Jewish religion, the highest insult is
to be called an ingrate, because ingrates close people's hearts. When you
extend yourself for others and they show no gratitude, you begin to

question whether you should have extended yourself at all. We all know how it feels to go out of our way to help someone in need and not receive so much as a thank-you. You feel abused. It's painful and you swear to yourself that you won't be such a sucker next time.

In Jewish values, however, gratitude is seen not only as the necessary recompense we offer those who have done things for us. Gratitude is also seen as the principal bulwark against sin.

Consider the story of Joseph, the adored youngest child of his father who enjoys a good life. But his older brothers are jealous and conspire to kill him. Thankfully they have a last-minute change of heart and decide to sell Joseph into slavery for twenty pieces of silver instead. Joseph winds up in the estate of Potiphar, a high-ranking officer in Pharaoh's court. There he proves himself capable and a hard worker, and eventually Potiphar gives him the job of overseeing the entire estate. And so Joseph goes about his business and is elevated to a position of privilege in the house. Apparently he develops some muscles along the way, because Potiphar's wife watches Joseph, likes what she sees, and announces that she's available for an affair. She's a Mrs. Robinson type—the original biblical cougar. She badgers him to lie with her. Anytime Joseph wants sex, he just needs to let her know. But Joseph refuses.

Now, what stops him? A shallow understanding of this story would have it that we're supposed to admire Joseph's Boy Scout purity. How impressive! He *didn't* want to have sex with an attractive older woman! I don't know about you but that explanation bores me to tears. A deeper understanding of this story, however, can change a life. What stops Joseph from having an affair is not control over his libido. It's not fear of G-d. What he says to her is, *Your husband has been so good to me. How could I do that to him?* The story of Joseph and Potiphar's wife establishes gratitude as the antidote to sin.

Just imagine if the men who have been involved in so many recent sexual scandals had simply thought of all the good their wives do for them. So much humiliation and hurt would have been averted. If Tiger Woods had simply thought of the gratitude he owed Elin for marrying him, having his kids, taking care of them, and being devoted to their family, he would not have ruined his life.

Gratitude is the blessing that prevents us from becoming crooked. The source of all human corruption is an absence of gratitude. And once someone fully understands the power of gratitude and the depths to which it can and must reach, they'll never be the same again. Gratitude is the bedrock of a life of conscience, and an essential component to world redemption, and that's why it's a central Jewish value.

We see its power in our own homes. When do kids start going off the path? When do they start fighting with their parents, arguing with their siblings, and sowing discord? It's when they start ignoring all the things their parents do for them, when they decide that their parents' efforts are irrelevant or even unwelcome. Their attitude becomes *So you feed, clothe, shelter, and educate me? Not good enough. What else you got? I could use a car, and maybe spring break in Florida.* Teenage rebellion is at its root a function of ingratitude, though this does not excuse whatever flaws there may be in our parenting. But imperfect as we are, our kids should still put that all into the context of the tremendous sacrifices we make on their behalf.

That biblical commandment to honor your father and mother is really a simple commandment about gratitude. That it's part of the Ten Commandments ought to tell us something. Think about it—*honor your father and your mother.* Does that really seem like one of *the* most important rules of existence? That it should rank up there with "Do not kill"? With "I am the Lord your G-d"? The Ten Commandments doesn't even tell us to love our spouse! But the commandment to honor one's parents is there to demonstrate the fundamental importance of appreciation. We are commanded to acknowledge all that people do for us—even when we didn't ask for it, even when they have failed us in other areas, even if their gifts are given with somewhat selfish motivations. The typical teen response of

"Well, I didn't ask to be born!" is irrelevant. None of this matters. If you cannot honor your parents, your ability to honor the rest of creation will be hampered, as will your ability to enjoy life.

Gratitude is like a meat tenderizer. It softens us. It humanizes us. It makes us feel. It keeps us human.

When we show gratitude, suddenly we're grateful to G-d. When we're grateful to G-d, we cannot become corrupt. Corruption is a form of forgetfulness. When Barack Obama accepted his Nobel Peace Prize, he said to Europe, *You gave me this prize because I'm not George W. Bush and you didn't like his approach to military intervention. Now, I've just sent 30,000 more U.S. troops to Afghanistan, so perhaps you were hasty in your judgment of me as a bringer of peace when I believe that the times call for fighting terrorism.* But it was American arms that kept Europe free when Hitler overran the continent. *Don't forget that,* Obama said. *Show some gratitude to the American boys who never came home and are buried on European soil.* He warned them against forgetfulness and a lack of gratitude.

When we remember the good that people do for us, it affects *our* behavior. What would have saved John Edwards? If he had thought for only one moment, he would have remembered some simple truths. Here was a woman who had taken his last name, who had given him beautiful children, and who had given up her own career to campaign for him around the country, even as she was battling incurable cancer. Simple gratitude would tell him that hurting her and introducing her to public humiliation was simply out of the question.

Gratitude is intensely powerful. The Jewish obligation to gratitude extends so far, in fact, that it includes inanimate objects. Read about the Ten Plagues of Egypt and you'll notice something peculiar. Moses does not enact the first three plagues himself but instead instructs Aaron to. In order: Moses does not transform the Nile River into blood or bring forth the frogs from the Nile, but Aaron does. When G-d says to Moses, "Stretch out thy rod, and smite the dust of the land, that it may become lice throughout all the land of Egypt," again it is Aaron who turns all of

Egypt's dust into lice. Moses enacts the next seven plagues, so why not these first three? Because the water of the Nile and the dust of Egypt saved his life. When he was an infant and placed in a basket, the water delivered him to safety. When he killed an Egyptian man he'd witnessed strike a Jewish man, he buried that man in the sand and thus was spared punishment. And now he simply couldn't show ingratitude to the water and the dust, because to do so would put his character at risk.

Even more remarkable? It wasn't even the same water. Rivers run. It wasn't the same water that had saved Moses so many years earlier. From a purely intellectual point of view, this would seem to make no sense.

This doesn't make sense on a purely intellectual level but we are not, and were never meant to be, purely intellectual beings. Let me give you another example. My parents fought a lot when I was a boy. Some of these arguments were very traumatic. We had very little money and my father drove a beat-up old white truck that he used to deliver material. This truck was always breaking down, and the resultant stress created a lot of tension in the house. My father called one night to say that the truck had broken down again. We couldn't afford a tow truck. He needed my mother to come meet him with her car, drive her car behind the truck, and push him home. So she drove out, and I remember waiting for them to come back. Was it going to be a calm night or an argumentative one? Suddenly, after half an hour, they pulled up. Both cars were home safely and everyone went inside, and all was calm. I was about six years old at the time. And I was so grateful that I walked out to my mother's car and kissed the front fender.

An embarrassing recollection? Not at all. Judaism conditions us to be sensitive to all walks of life—even things that have no life. If we are so sensitive that we can appreciate the blessing of a functioning automobile, if we are grateful for every person and every *thing* that brings peace and comfort to our home, we decrease our risk of becoming callous and entitled.

Gratitude is what most establishes our humanity. Gratitude means that you have the capacity to be touched by the kindness of others. Think of what it means to be touched. When you're touched, it leaves an imprint. It leaves a mark. But if you're made of steel or of stone, you're unmarked. And that's exactly what we mean when we say someone is acting inhuman. We're saying that they behave as if nothing touches them. They're cold and unfeeling. In a word—ungrateful.

Gratitude is also the beginning of a true relationship because it opens people's hearts. Gratitude ensures that when you do something for someone, it's not forgotten. When I was a young rabbi working with students at Oxford University, I was so idealistic, so driven, so energetic. I wore myself out, speaking, teaching, and opening my home to these students. I gave my whole self to these students. My family suffered because I was gone so often, trying to raise money to keep the student organization in the black. It was exhausting but I wanted to do everything I could for them.

Then when my students graduated, many of them went on to get great jobs. They'd graduated from the best university in England, so they pretty much got to choose their landing spot. Of course many chose big banks and securities firms—Solomon Brothers, Merrill Lynch, Bank of America, the list goes on. They started drawing huge salaries plus year-end bonuses. These men and women in their mid-twenties were making upward of $250,000 a year. So I would ask them if perhaps they wanted to support the organization now that they were in a position to do so? And they would say, sure, Shmuley, of course, glad to! Four weeks later I would receive a check for $50. They were buying BMWs and skiing in the Swiss Alps, but when it came to giving back to the organization that had sustained them throughout their lean student years, $50 was all they could muster. This was less than what they would spend on a typical Saturday night dinner.

My heart started to close. When you don't show gratitude, people begin to think to themselves, "Gosh, I'm a sucker." They start to think that they were stupid for extending themselves toward you. They start to wonder if perhaps they were too generous, or if perhaps they were wrong to give to you in the first place! Ingratitude sends people into a psychological tailspin because it profoundly denies the graciousness they tried to demonstrate. When you're ungrateful, you increase the psychic burden on other people. Now *they* have a harder time meeting *their* obligation to be grateful. I certainly had a hard time being grateful for that $50 when I knew my former students could afford something respectable for an organization that had spent so much on them.

It's really quite simple. The less gratitude there is in the world, the less goodness.

Think of what the expression means—to be spoiled. "Spoiled" is really quite an accurate term for what happens to children who can neither experience nor express gratitude. Say I take my kid on a trip with me to Paris, and they've been on many trips, so this particular trip doesn't seem out of the ordinary, and their response to it is essentially, "Oh, that's nice," and then they yawn and go back to staring out the window. Not only does that mean they're spoiled, it means that something deep inside has been lost. It means that no matter what I do, I can't touch my own child with my love and kindness.

Entitlement, which is essentially ingratitude, lessens a child's ability to experience joy. This is why as parents we need to be on guard against overwhelming our kids' natural capacity for incredible joy with too much stuff that is too easily obtained. If we give them everything, they will appreciate nothing. Parents today live with an overwhelming sense of guilt. Many don't spend enough time with their kids, so they try to compensate with material goods. But it doesn't work, and the result is a home that is both less harmonious and less attuned to the beauty of everyday life.

True character is always built on a foundation of gratitude. I have always hated the expression "give back." You hear this a lot, particularly around the holidays, or when someone has struck it very rich and has made the decision to contribute to charity or to become a full-blown philanthropist. They're "giving back," they'll say. What a condescending expression. It's so arrogant. It makes it sound as if the giver has ascended to such great heights and now, looking down at the little people, will part with a small portion of his or her fortune to help other people out.

But gratitude is not about the haves condescending to the have-nots. Rather, it's the haves retaining their humanity even as they climb the social ladder. It's about them never forgetting how many people made their success possible: parents who supported them in their darkest hours, teachers who inspired them to work harder, friends who gave love and encouragement. You're not giving back to these people. *They helped to create you. You owe your success to them.* None of us ever achieves anything of significance on our own. We all have to remember, and repay, the debt of gratitude that accounts for our success.

CHAPTER 9

Unity

With an eye made quiet by the power of harmony, and the deep power of joy, we see into the life of things.

—WILLIAM WORDSWORTH

Life's errors cry for the merciful beauty that can modulate their isolation into a harmony with the whole.

—RABINDRANATH TAGORE

The classic formula of the Jewish faith is *Shema Yisrael:* "Hear O Israel, the Lord is our G-d, the Lord is One."

The Jewish concept of G-d is that G-d is one, and that He is unified, possessing no parts, and is the source of all existence. He is Creator of heaven and earth, the source of light and darkness, even what appears to us as evil. "I form light and create darkness," we read in Isaiah 45:7. "I am the Lord who does all these things." Rabbi Shneur Zalman of Liadi, founder of Chabad Hassidism, took this a dramatic step further by saying that nothing in all existence other than G-d is real. Everything exists within G-d and the goal of life is to annihilate the sense of separateness we sometimes feel from Him.

I try to remember this whenever the fractured nature of contemporary life starts to fray my nerves. The unity of G-d becomes a Jewish value with real application for our daily existence because it asserts that rather than just living in the heavens, G-d controls all events here on earth, and so we must reject dualism. There is one G-d and He is everywhere. It's all holy. Both heaven and earth emanate from the same source.

This is what makes Judaism an ideal spiritual model for a generation that seems torn between what they know to be right and what feels good. Their minds and hearts send them in separate directions. Men and women don't seem to understand one another. Nations and religions continue to fight. But unity promises that we're not from different planets and we're not from different deities. We are all children of our Creator. The blatant inequality of humankind is glaring—some people are richer than others, some are taller, some are brighter, and some are prettier. But all of that pales in significance beside this awesome idea of all stemming from a common origin. We're all from the same place and we can create harmony and unity.

Unity suggests that all conflicts can be resolved. It suggests that those with out-of-control passions can rein them in. It suggests that you don't have to be at war with yourself. It implies that your mind and heart need not pull you in different directions. That your legitimate personal and ego needs can dovetail with your selfless, communal responsibilities. That your individual self can live within a relationship where that self is shared with another.

What was also revolutionary about the Jewish idea of a single, unified, indivisible G-d was its suggestion of unity *within* creation. Does everything reduce to one essential point that encompasses all organic and inorganic matter, every idea, and every person? Or is everything detached and unrelated? Is the world made up of puzzle pieces that ultimately yield a single portrait, or is it chaos? People have debated these questions for centuries.

Ancient people knew enough of their own limitations to pay homage to lofty powers in the universe that they deemed responsible for the ordering of life. Uncorrupted by the shallow distractions so common in modern life, they had an intuition for the transcendental. They accounted for the varied wonders of nature by postulating the existence of many gods. There was a god of lightning, a god of the oceans, a god for men, and a separate god for women. But then along came Abraham, who professed the existence of a G-d none could see, creator of the universe and governor of all that happened on earth.

According to the Talmud, Abraham put forward the idea that all existence emanated from a single source by a process of logical deduction. At first, witnessing the brightness and brilliance of the sun, how its warmth animates all life, Abraham prostrated himself before its rays and worshipped it as the supreme deity. But in the evening, the moon, which seemed much less impressive by comparison, launched a rebellion, assisted by the heavenly host of the stars, and defeated the sun, and the earth was shrouded in darkness. Abraham then worshipped the moon as the conqueror of the sun.

But in the morning, when the sun rallied its forces and reestablished its preeminence in the skies, Abraham rejected each as canceling the other out, and he turned to the other forces of nature in his search for the ultimate deity. He began to worship the air, the all-encompassing ether. It was everywhere. Surely it must be the great divinity he sought. But he then pondered the human superiority to the air, since humans, though porous and having bodily cavities, were still able to contain air and breathe, thus proving that they were its master. But having witnessed man's propensity for making huge blunders, Abraham was not about to worship himself or any other man. It was then that the great truth dawned upon him: The deity was an all-encompassing being who transcended nature but also made up its fabric and served as its underlying, invisible essence. Abraham began to understand that all of nature was a veil that masked the presence of the deity, and that people must learn to find the G-d who was hidden in nature.

Wow. This was revolutionary. The universe had no competing powers. Nor had G-d created the universe and abandoned it to its own laws. G-d was personal and present. Says 1 Chronicles 29:11–12: "All things belong to Him, and He is the Lord of all." The pagan notion of demonic forces that wage war against the deities is, therefore, wholly alien to biblical values. Even Satan, the Bible says, is no more than the heavenly prosecutor, serving the divine purpose. The Zohar sees Satan as a divine agent, whose mission is to exercise every charm in human seduction, thereby providing humans with choice. G-d wants to be special. He want us to choose Him, and not because there is no other possibility. In understanding the role of Satan, the Zohar gives the analogy of a prostitute the king sends to test the moral stamina of his son, the crown prince. Even while employing all her guile to corrupt the prince, the harlot hopes he will not succumb. His fate, however, is entirely dependent on exercising good judgment.

Good and evil do not represent different and contending kingdoms. Both emanate from the one true G-d, which is why theodicy—the reconciliation of the good G-d and the existence of evil—has always been a problem for Jews. We do not excuse evil as emanating from a source outside G-d. We don't conveniently blame all bad things on the devil. There is no cosmic strife between opposing forces. By the same token, humankind constitutes a single family, all nations emanating from the same source. Adam is the human father of all men. At the end of days, the human family will be reunited in an era of eternal brotherhood (Isaiah 2:2–4).

G-d's unity has a direct bearing on our daily lives in that Judaism maintains that we, like the world around us, can integrate all our diverse impulses into one effective system. We need not feel torn apart by the conflicting impulses of intellect and emotion. In the same way the world at large is not diffuse, neither is the human soul. We can get it together.

Once on an airplane a young doctor, who turned out to be Jewish, asked me what I was doing. I was putting my tefillin on my arm and head to say my morning prayers, and he had never seen tefillin before. I said to him, "I'm a rabbi. But I'm also a relationship counselor. And I've learned something. Most of the people who come to me who've messed up their lives have a common denominator. Whatever the reason they're coming, it comes down to this. Somewhere along the line their heart and their head stopped communicating. The things the mind knew to be correct were never transmitted to the heart. There was a blockage of some sort. Or the reverse was true. The heart felt some heated passion for something. But the message was not sent back to the head to scrutinize that thing—like an illicit relationship—to determine if it was good or bad. So I put on tefillin each morning, as commanded by the Bible, in order to have a daily meditation of my heart and mind acting in unison. One box goes on my hand against my heart, the other on my head. And I get them aligned and in sync so they behave that way throughout the day."

In short, we are not meant to have different parts of ourselves at war with one another. We humans are supposed to be one unified system.

Judaism is a religion of life. It rejects the belief that G-d occupies the heavens and shuns the earth. Isaiah declares, "Holy, holy, holy is the Lord of Hosts; the whole earth is full of His glory." It is in *this* world that G-d is to be found, and it is in *this* world that man must live a G-dly life. Holiness must pervade his every action, for no realm of existence is outside G-d's dominion. A rejection of the physical world is a rejection of G-d's omnipresence. The great medieval Jewish philosopher Rabbi Judah Halevi wrote in his magnum opus, the Kuzari: "The servant of G-d does not withdraw himself from secular contact lest he be a burden to the world and the world to him; he does not hate life, which is one of G-d's bounties granted to him. . . . On the contrary, he loves this world and wishes for a long life."

The objective of life from a Jewish perspective is to draw close to G-d, not by ascending to the heavens, but by causing G-d to dwell here on earth. Far from rejecting physical existence, Judaism views all of creation as having a potential for holiness. The Ten Commandments, given by G-d on tablets of stone, illustrate the majestic scope of G-d's demands and man's mission. They soar from the most basic "I am the Lord your G-d" to embrace the whole gamut of human existence. Even thoughts are included: "Thou shalt not covet." This was the work that was inaugurated by Abraham. Rabbinical legend tells of a heavenly dispute in which the angels asked G-d why He had forsaken them in favor of Abraham. The Almighty responded, "You angels made Me Master over the heavens, where I have always been King. But Abraham made Me Master over the earth, where previously I was unknown."

Just think of the possibilities. I know people who have given up. They hit forty or fifty and they're bitter and cynical. They've been through a divorce and they swear they'll never get married again. They had a miserable childhood and they swear they'll never have kids. They were fired from a job and now they think that people are mean and untrustworthy. Yes, we all get wounded. But before you decide the world is a place of misery and loneliness, what about your responsibility to unearth its G-dly nature? There is so much hidden light waiting to be discovered. There are lonely people who are seeking that one person who hasn't given up. There are teenagers waiting to be inspired. There are firms waiting for a sensitive and giving employee like you. So why have you thrown in the towel and assumed that only in heaven will you find peace?

I was once sitting with an elderly woman who was very depressed that her children were fighting. She said, "I wish I were dead," and she looked like she meant it. I comforted her and said, "What makes you think that death is any better than life?"

You want peace? We have to create it here on earth. Stop searching for G-d in the graveyard and stop looking for Him in heaven. He is just as much here as He is there. Find G-d in every leaf, in every blade of grass, in the smiles of your children, in the tenderness of your spouse. Act as His agent, in the comfort you give friends and in the bread you give to the poor. In the elderly woman's case, I told her she could use her influence to heal the family and bring her children closer together. I told her I would help her. But death was an escape that would solve nothing.

I personally have little interest in the heavens. What I could I possibly find there of interest—angels? They're perfect. What would they need from me? I would feel superfluous, useless. I am trying to figure out my life here on earth. And would I really want a heaven that was nothing but an escape from earth? Is heaven just something I fall back on because I failed in life down here? No, I have to work to create harmony and unity down here. I have to learn to act in accordance with my convictions. There can't be two of me. I have to work to be always loving toward my wife. I have to learn how to talk to my children. And I have to learn to listen.

Unity means that you should become a peace-seeker. The Talmud says, "Always be like the students of Aaron, who love peace and pursue peace." Wow. *Pursue* peace. Don't wait for it to find you. Go out and create it.

I am a Jew, but all of G-d's children are my brothers and sisters. Christians and Muslims, atheists and agnostics, Hindus and Buddhists, Native Americans and native Pakistanis. I can be committed to my tradition and my country, the great United States, without impeding my ability to be just as close to people who seem distant from me. Underneath it all, we are all one. So go out and befriend someone. Give them dignity. Give them your time. A compliment. Make them feel special.

Don't just get into that taxicab and rush onto your cell phone. Say hello. Make some conversation. The cab driver wasn't created by G-d to drive you from point A to point B. He is your human brother, with his own dreams and aspirations. Make him feel your heart.

Knowing that there is an underlying unity to life obligates us to always seek harmony. I once met a teenage girl whose life was threatened by anorexia. She hated her appearance and thought that every morsel of food made her fat. I spent days explaining to her that the beauty of the body and the beauty of the soul worked in harmony. She had to heal one to heal the other. And if she was putting her soul in jeopardy, her body could never reflect its light. Nothing, not even our own bodies, exists outside G-d.

CHAPTER 10

Defending Human Life

∞∞∞∞∞∞∞∞∞∞∞∞

*If I choose to bless another person, I will always
end up feeling more blessed.*
——MARIANNE WILLIAMSON

*The happiest people I have known have been
those who gave themselves no concern about their
own souls, but did their uttermost to mitigate the
miseries of others.*
——ELIZABETH CADY STANTON

M y wife and I are blessed with nine children. And I hate it when
my kids fight. If one of my children breaks something in the
house, I may not be amused. But I am far angrier if he or she blames it
on a sibling. Yes, the information is useful. But it's also dispiriting. Once
while on vacation, we took the children for ice cream. My second oldest
daughter pulled her sister's hair, and I told her I would not be taking her
inside the store unless she apologized. She refused. "Then you'll stay in
the car," I told her, whereupon her older sister, the innocent victim, began

to cry that her sister hadn't meant it and that she would not go into the ice cream store without her. Wow. That felt good!

If one could briefly summarize the vast contribution made to Jewish thought by the Rabbi Israel Baal Shem Tov and Hassidism over the past three hundred years, it would be that Hassidism taught us that in our efforts to be close to G-d, we must put others before us, at times even before G-d. In the Bible G-d continually exhorts us to defend the oppressed and to show special sensitivity to widows and orphans.

So I tell my kids all the time that our principal purpose in life is to love G-d and to love His children. G-d is all-powerful, but people are not. G-d is not in need of our defense. Humans, however, are. As the Baal Shem Tov said, love for G-d is shown mainly through one's devotion to one's fellow man. All parents love their children more than they love themselves. The G-d of Israel is no different. What G-d principally desires from us is not to defend Him, but to care for and love his creatures. Indeed, the laws that regulate our treatment of each other account for a substantial portion of the Torah. Rabbi Akiva says that the commandment to "love your neighbor as yourself" (Leviticus 19:18) is "an all-encompassing principle of the Torah." And the great sage Hillel, when asked to sum up the entire Torah into one teaching, told a potential convert: "That which you hate, never do unto others. This is the entire Torah, the rest being but commentary. Now, go and study."

Maimonides, as mentioned earlier, in his epistle on martyrdom, sharply rebukes a contemporary twelfth-century rabbi's condemnation of Jews who were living in Spain during the Islamic Almohad persecutions, many of whom pondered converting to Islam rather than facing death by the sword. Maimonides goes to great lengths to show that G-d Himself rebuffed and even punished those who had condemned the people of Israel. He notes that Moses, Elijah, Isaiah, and even the ministering angels were chastised by G-d when they came to Him with reports that the Jews were sinful and had broken G-d's covenant. *They were telling the truth*. But so great was G-d's anger at Isaiah after he said, "I sit here in the midst of a nation who have defiled and profaned their lips [with prayers to idols]," that G-d sent an angel with a pan of coals to burn Isaiah's mouth.

But if Isaiah's allegations were true, why was he punished? And if Moses was correct in accusing the Jews of abandoning the path of G-d and assimilating into Egyptian culture, why was he rebuked for this accurate report? The reason is that it was not their function as prophets to indict the Jewish nation, but to correct them. G-d expected these great men to find merit rather than condemn. Their mandate was to defend their fellow humans rather than incriminate them. G-d alone is the judge of the earth.

We are bidden to serve as angels of mercy rather than prosecutors. G-d gives life and takes life. Humans protect life and defend life.

In fact, the outstanding figures of the Bible always interceded on human life's behalf. When G-d came to Abraham and informed him that He would destroy Sodom and Gomorrah, Abraham pleaded for them to be spared. That the most righteous man on the earth could challenge his Creator and defend the most wicked and entreat G-d for clemency is a remarkable example that we should all take to heart. If you are a biological or spiritual descendant of Abraham, then you cannot stand idly by and watch your neighbor suffer. That would betray what Abraham stood for.

Moses did not ask G-d to explain what good the Jews received from their enslavement. He simply demanded, in the strongest possible terms, that the Almighty bring their ordeal to an end. The Bible records that Moses, after smashing the two tablets into a thousand pieces, again ascended Mount Sinai to plead with G-d to forgive the Jews for the sin of the golden calf. "Now, if you will forgive the people," he said, "then good. But if you will not forgive their sin . . . blot me out, I pray you, from the Torah which you have written."

Wow. Is there any other story, in any literature claiming to be divine, where a human demands that the master of the universe remove his name from a divine work so that he will not be associated with a G-d who refuses to forgive? This is powerful stuff. I find it the most beautiful defense of human life ever recorded. Until the time that we, together with our Creator, abolish every form of pain from the earth, we must band together and comfort one another. Never should we witness a living creature's pain and remain silent.

To defend human life means not only joining the U.S. military and fighting for the weak—one of the value's highest expressions—but even simply trying to find good in people on a daily basis. A coworker says something a little nasty to you? Maybe she had a fight with her spouse at home. No need to have a whole other fight with her. Maybe she's in pain. Find good in her. Think about all the times she was nice to you.

The same is true when you see others suffering. Don't excuse their pain. Don't try to understand it. Your responsibility is to end it.

Early in 2010, my friend Pat Robertson said the people of Haiti were hit with an earthquake because in the nineteenth century they made a pact with the devil to push out the French. "Something happened a long time ago in Haiti, and people might not want to talk about it. They were under the heel of the French . . . and they got together and swore a pact to the devil. They said, 'We will serve you if you'll get us free from the French.' True story. And the devil said, 'OK, it's a deal.' Ever since, they have been cursed by one thing after another." When a nationally prominent minister of religion blames innocent victims for their own death at the hands of a natural disaster, the remark cannot go unchallenged.

First of all, how does Robertson know? More important, is this the purpose of a religious leader—to inflict the final indignity on 170,000 people who lost their lives, by accusing them of having deserved it? Does G-d really need Pat's defense? Or do these poor people, whose children were crushed under tons of rubble, need his compassion more than his condemnation?

Such comments are simply reprehensible, deplorable, and the absolute antithesis of the true biblical response to suffering. The Bible is replete with examples of individuals who witnessed the suffering of the innocent. And rather than blaming the victims, they always blamed G-d. When

Abraham was told by G-d that Sodom and Gomorrah would experience a natural disaster, he lifted his hands to the heavens and begged G-d for clemency. "I am but dust and ashes," Abraham said. But even a mere mortal like him had to protest G-d's plan, and he begged G-d to spare them. We have no idea why the people of Haiti have suffered so greatly, with four devastating hurricanes and a catastrophic earthquake in just a few years. But it had nothing to do with them deserving to suffer because of action taken by their ancestors.

What the Haitians did deserve is what we are *all* created for—long life, health, and happiness. Instead of treating a broken people with indignation and censure, we should be shaking the ramparts from the heavens asking for mercy from G-d.

It is not surprising that so many people today repudiate religion as a negative force due to inflammatory statements like Robertson's. Rest assured, this is not religion. Religion is the voice of love and compassion, not of censure and condemnation.

When a person is in pain, when there is a holocaust, we don't need fifty rabbis and priests pulling out their word processors and explaining how G-d is good despite what we are witnessing. Instead we need millions of people springing into action saving lives, alleviating anguish, and demanding from G-d better times. At the very least, let's not serve as the cause of pain to others. Let's ensure that the only tears our actions cause in the lives of our fellow humans are tears of joy. We must dedicate time and resources to charitable endeavors. We must counsel husbands and wives whose marriages are faltering, devote ourselves to medical research that prolongs life, and pray for those hurting from illness and disease. We have to get people to stop texting when they drive and to eat healthier. And we have to do everything possible to end war and to fight the people who constantly bring war until they're neutralized and peace can break out.

In the words of our father Abraham, when we witness people in pain, we should shake our fists to the heavens and demand of the Creator, "Will the Judge of the entire earth not practice justice?"

CHAPTER 11

Suffering Is Not Redemptive

I can sympathize with everything, except suffering.

—OSCAR WILDE

A laughing man is stronger than a suffering man.

—GUSTAVE FLAUBERT

After the Holocaust there were largely two camps. Many in the Orthodox community questioned G-d as to why it happened. But secular Zionists actually had a much more Jewish response. It was they who largely built the state of Israel. They rejected any theological justification or self-blame and worked even harder to create a state where Jews could finally find refuge and build an army to protect them from another genocide. The appropriate response to death is always life. And the Jewish response to suffering is to demand that G-d put an end to it.

So many people search for a reason why people suffer. They want to redeem suffering in some way. They want to give it meaning. They cannot accept that it carries no purpose. *Suffering ennobles the spirit*, these people say. *It makes you more mature. It focuses you on what's really important in life.*

Alternatively, they want to see suffering as punishment for sin, a sentiment that is pervasive among many religious people. Right after the Haitian earthquake that killed 230,000 people, I traveled to Port-au-Prince on a relief mission to visit the orphanages there. When I returned I gave a public lecture designed to highlight the devastation I had witnessed and galvanize people to help. I also addressed the issue of why a good G-d allows the innocent to suffer. I was amazed when an observant Jew approached me to say that the people of Haiti were not innocent, immersed as they are in voodoo and idol-worship. "Surely you don't mean to say that the morgue filled with the babies that I witnessed, the stench so bad that I was gagging, deserved to die? Or that the discarded bodies I saw being eaten by scavenging dogs deserved their fate?" His response: The people of Haiti as a whole were punished. A similar sentiment had earlier been voiced by the Reverend Pat Robertson on *The 700 Club*.

I have always been puzzled as to why many religious people enjoy portraying G-d as executioner-in-chief and are always finding reasons to justify human suffering.

I would argue that suffering has no point, no redeeming qualities, and any attempts to infuse it with rich significance are wrongheaded.

I am not saying that suffering can't lead to good things. It can. The rich man who has contempt for the poor and suddenly loses his money can become more empathetic when he himself starts struggling to make ends meet. The arrogant executive who treats her subordinates like dirt can soften when she is told she has breast cancer.

But does it have to come about this way? Is suffering the only way to learn goodness? Jewish values maintain that there is no good that comes from suffering that could not have come about through a more blessed means. Some people win the lottery and are so humbled by their good fortune that they dedicate a huge portion to charity. A rock star like Bono becomes rich and famous and dedicates his celebrity to relieving poverty. You don't have to suffer to learn goodness. Yes, the Holocaust led directly to the creation of the state of Israel. But plenty of nations came into existence without any gas chambers.

It irritates me to hear people speak of how much they have learned from hardship and suffering—as if similar lessons could not have been acquired through pleasant means.

Here is another way Jewish values are so strongly distinguished from others. Virtually every religion and values system believes that suffering is redemptive. In Christianity, the suffering servant, the crucified Christ, atones for the sins of mankind through his own torment. The message: no suffering, no redemption. Someone has to die so the sins of mankind are erased. According to Christianity, if Jesus had not suffered and died on the cross, we would all be damned for our sins. Suffering is therefore extolled in Romans in the New Testament: "And not only that, but we also boast in our sufferings, knowing that suffering produces endurance, and endurance produces character, and character produces hope." In 2 Corinthians: "If we are being afflicted, it is for your consolation and salvation; if we are being consoled, it is for your consolation, which you experience when you patiently endure the same sufferings that we are also suffering." Indeed, Paul even made suffering an obligation, encouraging the fledging Christians to "share in suffering like a good soldier of Christ Jesus."

According to Judaism, there are no ennobling qualities in pain. I believe that not only is suffering not redemptive, it is downright destructive. *Suffering isn't a blessing, it's a curse.* It leaves you bitter rather than blessed, scarred rather than humble. Few endure suffering without serious and lasting trauma. Suffering leads to a tortured spirit and a pessimistic outlook on life. It scars our psyches and creates a cynical consciousness, devoid and bereft of hope. Suffering causes us to dig out the insincerity in the hearts of our fellows and to be envious of other people's happiness. If individuals do become better people as a result of their suffering, it is *despite* the fact that they suffered, not because of it. Ennoblement of character comes through triumph over suffering, rather than its endurance.

Several years ago I was privileged to meet former Beirut hostage Brian Keenan. He was in great pain and yet he maintained a warm and beautiful smile and wrote something extremely witty in his dedication to my copy of his book, the account of his ordeal as a hostage for so many years. After speaking with him for some time, I came to realize the special qualities he possessed—his love for others, his warmth, earthiness, and optimistic view of life—had been present prior to his ordeal. He did not gain them because he suffered. His greatness lay in the fact that he retained these beautiful traits *despite* having suffered. Speak to a Holocaust survivor like Elie Wiesel and ask what he gathered from his suffering, aside from loneliness, heartbreak, and misery. To be sure, he also learned the value of life and the sublime quality of human companionship. Wiesel is an incredibly profound man. But these lessons, this depth, could easily have been learned through life-affirming experiences that do not leave permanent scars on the psyche.

I believe my parents' divorce drove me to a deeper understanding of life and a greater embrace of religion. And yet I know people who have led completely privileged lives and have deeper philosophies of life and are even more devoted to Jewish values than I. And they have the advantage of not being bitter, cynical, or pessimistic the way I can sometimes be because of the pain of my early childhood. When I served for eleven years as rabbi at Oxford University, I noticed that the college students I knew who were raised in homes in which their parents gave them huge amounts of love and attention were the most healthy and balanced of all. They were usually also the best scholars. Those who were neglected or demeaned by their parents could also be positive and loving, but first a Herculean effort was needed to undo the emotional scarring.

Whatever good we as individuals, or the world in general, receive from suffering can be brought about in a painless, joyful manner.

When a person protests to G-d, it is not a challenge to divine providence, because we are not challenging G-d's authority or asserting that
He has visited cruelty or injustice upon humanity. Neither are we maintaining that G-d's plans have gone askew. Rather, what we are saying is
this: *We believe that somehow this must be to our benefit and that You are a
good and just Creator. But You are also all-powerful, and would it not therefore
be possible for You to bring about this desired end by less painful means?* We
are asking G-d to change the means He employs to achieve His always
just and noble ends. To those who argue that suffering humbles the heart
and ennobles the spirit, I would ask if they then pray to the Almighty
that He visit even greater suffering on mankind so as to induce further
ethical merit?

In this aspect, Jewish values are set apart. The very essence of the
Christian faith is that humans were so hopelessly sinful that the only
chance they had for salvation was for G-d to send His only son to die on
the cross. Without blood, there is no atonement. Likewise, in Islam we
often hear that to get into heaven one must give one's life as a jihadist.
Life must be sacrificed.

It's interesting to me that Christians believe that this concept of no
atonement without blood comes from Judaism and the Bible's prescrip-
tion of sacrifice. First of all, human sacrifice is labeled an outright abomination throughout the Bible. More important, animal sacrifice is just one
of many avenues in the Bible toward forgiveness of sin. Those who could
not afford an animal brought flour offerings. But the highest form of
atonement came not from any kind of sacrifice at all but from repentance.
The most famous story of forgiveness in the entire Bible is that of Jonah
and the whale and the salvation of the city of Nineveh. Not one animal
is sacrificed and absolutely no blood is spilled. The people simply repent
of their evil ways.

Nobody has to die so that others might live. And we don't need suffering to teach us to value the important things in life. Misguided notions

like these have allowed humans to excuse suffering and allow it to linger when our divine mandate is to get rid of it completely.

But here is my greatest proof that deep down, none of us believe that suffering is redemptive. The thing we love most in the whole world is our children. How many of us purposely inflict suffering on our kids in order to refine their character? On the contrary, we do everything possible to prevent our kids' suffering because we cannot bear to see them in pain and because we know how deeply injurious it is to their well-being.

The existence of suffering is the greatest challenge to faith because it seems to undermine its central premise: that G-d exists, that He is good, and that He loves humanity. The staggering number of people killed in the wars and genocides of the twentieth century led many to believe that we were alone in the universe. Or worse, if G-d does exist and just stood by as Hitler, Stalin, Mao, and Pol Pot flourished, then why pray? Of what use is a Creator who, having called man into existence, subsequently abandons him to fate and the elements?

The Jewish tradition of challenging G-d is absolutely central to answering this question. Most religions would see challenging G-d as blasphemy. They deal with the problem of suffering by blaming human sin. Why do people suffer? Simple. They deserve it. They have done bad things, so G-d punishes them. Or their ancestors did bad things and the iniquity of the parents is being visited upon the children. Or—another classic response—what appears to be suffering is nothing of the sort. Really it's something good even though it comes in a very bitter pill.

But in Judaism challenging G-d is a religious obligation. Human beings have a right to health and financial sustenance, without which they cannot happily serve G-d. Those who lie in hospital beds or have lost a child harbor too broken a spirit to offer meaningful service to their Creator. We have a right to a happy life. That's why Jewish values emphasize the right of humans to complain to G-d when they needlessly suffer. We don't seek a response to suffering so much as its alleviation.

G-d wants us to challenge every form of suffering and therefore, through torture, inquisitions, pogroms, crusades, massacres, and the Holocaust, the Jewish spirit has never broken and the Jewish flame has never been extinguished. Through every plague G-d has visited on the earth's inhabitants, the threefold Jewish response has been (1) to beseech and demand from G-d a cessation of the plague; (2) to devote their energies, through medicine and technology, to finding a cure; and (3) to pray for the speedy arrival of the Messiah, who would bring redemption to mankind and an end to the earth's imperfections.

As human beings, it is not our role to concern ourselves with G-d's affairs or to justify His actions by saying that the suffering of other people carries an internal, albeit latent, good. Why G-d brings suffering upon mankind, especially on the righteous, transcends human comprehension. Moreover, it is none of our business. G-d must pursue His plan. But human beings are charged with the eternal pursuit of love and justice, even if it means sparring with the Creator. These are two legitimate roles that may often conflict. The moral imperative beholden upon us when we witness another individual's suffering is to cause it to cease, not to attempt to understand it ourselves or explain it to others.

The question to pose when righteous people suffer is not, "Please, G-d, explain to us why bad things happen and how it fits into Your overall plan for creation," but rather: "Master of the Universe, how could You allow this to happen? Was it not You who taught us in Your magnificent Torah that life is sacred and must be preserved at all costs? Where is that life now? Was is not You who promised that the good deserve goodness and not pain? Where is your promise now? By everything that is sacred to You, I demand that this cease." Far from being an affront to divine authority, these words are part of the human mandate. Remaining passive in the face of human suffering is a sin against both man and the Creator.

British author C. S. Lewis, in the biographical movie *Shadowlands,* embraces a position of Christian acquiescence as the proper response to suffering. The classic dualist approach maintains that suffering is necessary to distinguish between pain and happiness. Lewis's dying wife (Joy Davidson, who is in fact Jewish) tells him that the happiness they experience together now, that she is alive and they are married, is directly dependent on the impending tragedy of her death. He accepts this position as long as she is alive, but as soon as she dies, the once submissive Lewis becomes angry with the religious platitudes offered by his friend, a doctor of divinity. He shouts and orders the minister to be silent, swinging his cudgel at the thought that G-d could somehow desire anyone's death, especially a good person who had caused no one harm.

I sympathize entirely with this response, not because Lewis was pained and was thus incapable of submitting to the will of G-d at that moment, but rather because his wife, like every decent human being, deserved a long and happy life and was promised one by the Almighty Creator. How could this cleric be so sanctimonious and arrogant as to dismiss the death of someone else's beloved in the belief that it carried with it a cosmic reason? The Garden of Eden, the perfect world G-d created, had no suffering. This proves that perfection is tied to a decided lack of suffering. Let us cease thinking that suffering is beneficent.

The sin of justifying human suffering is especially heinous for a rabbi because it betrays a fundamental ignorance of Jewish values. Judaism sees death, illness, and suffering as aberrations brought about through the sin of Adam in Eden. G-d placed Adam and Eve in His garden and told them they were permitted to eat from all the trees but one. "And the Lord G-d commanded the man saying, Of every tree of the garden you may eat; But of the tree of the knowledge of good and evil, you shall not eat from it; for on the day that you eat from it you shall surely die." The verse is puzzling. Adam and Eve did indeed eat from the tree of knowledge, yet they did not die on that day. In fact, Adam lived on for more than nine hundred years! How can we account for this discrepancy?

According to the Jewish interpretation, the meaning of the verse was that Adam lost his immortality on the day he ate of the tree of knowledge.

As G-d's direct handiwork, created in His direct image, man was never meant to experience death. Man was meant to live eternally. And as long as Adam remained attached to the infinite source of life, he was eternal like his Creator. By sinning against G-d, Adam and Eve severed themselves from the infinite source of life and immediately began to decay and die. Through his transgression, Adam lived many more years, but one day he succumbed to death, just as every apple succumbs to decay when detached from a tree.

The implications of this rabbinical teaching on this crucial passage of Genesis are profound. There was never meant to be a place for death in our world, and neither was there a plan for life to include suffering or pain. The Garden of Eden, previously this earth, was perfect. This rabbinical teaching also declares that suffering has no meaning. As it was never part of the original plan, it has no purpose. It was a mistake to be corrected, a crooked line that can still be made straight. No human was ever predestined to suffer. Neither will any form of misery be present in the perfect messianic age that has been promised for three millennia by the Almighty through His prophets and sages. Only now, in this interim period between life in Eden and life in the perfect world to come, are we ravaged by cancer, AIDS, car crashes, hatred, and genocide.

Man's mission was never to make peace with suffering and death, but to abolish them from the face of the earth for all eternity by joining G-d as a junior partner in creation. By challenging G-d whenever humans suffer, we do not degrade G-d but glorify Him to the highest heavens. We demonstrate that His teachings in the Torah about love, compassion, and togetherness have had an impact upon us. By studying medicine and offering aid to people in need, we live up to our highest calling of having been created in the divine image. The atheist doctor who struggles to cure AIDS is infinitely more in tune with Jewish values than the rabbi who tells his flock that suffering is part of the divine plan. The sinning businessman who may have never stepped into a synagogue but makes a loan to a colleague to save him from bankruptcy is more in tune with Jewish values' response to suffering than the rabbi who seeks to rationalize why children die of leukemia.

Our role as humans is not to give meaning to aberrations, but to heal them with G-dly light. Human beings are commanded by G-d to occupy themselves with life, never with death. Our energy must be dedicated not to explaining hurt and pain, but to combating them and to healing wounds.

We must act like the human body's immune system. Whenever the immune system senses even the tiniest germ, it declares war on the alien presence threatening the body's health. It is not the purpose of the body's immune system to understand why the body suffers. When a person begins to feel ill, it is not the mind that is first kicked into gear, searching for reasons. No, it is the body's immune system that jumps into action, ridding the body of the harmful bacillus. There is no deep reason for the germ. It simply must be eradicated.

CHAPTER 12

No Love Without Law

It may be true that the law cannot make a man love me, but it can keep him from lynching me, and I think that's pretty important.
—MARTIN LUTHER KING JR.

They do not love that do not show their love.
—WILLIAM SHAKESPEARE

Franz Kafka penned his father a letter the older man never read because he died before it reached him. The letter read in part, "It would have been thinkable that we might both have found each other in Judaism or that we might have begun from there in harmony. But what sort of Judaism was it that I got from you? . . . It was impossible to make a child, over-acutely observant from sheer nervousness, understand that the few flimsy gestures you performed in the name of Judaism, and with an indifference in keeping with their flimsiness, could have any higher meaning. For you they had meaning as little souvenirs of earlier times, and that is why you wanted to pass them on to me. But since they no longer had any intrinsic value, even for you, you could do this only through persuasion or threat."

These lines could be written by almost any child growing up in a Jewish or Christian home for whom religion has become a burden rather than a living spring. This happens when people forget that the purpose of religious ritual is to inculcate values. They come to think that divine laws consist of flimsy gestures and dusty moral codes irrelevant to the task of living a good and humane life. *Where's the passion,* they ask? *What's the point of following these arcane rules?*

Judaism in particular has often been accused by Christianity of being weighed down by legalism. Many Christians feel that their faith enables them to take spiritual flight while Jews remain tied down with excessive law and ritual. In the book of Romans, Paul even attacked the law as an impediment to true righteousness: "Therefore no one will be declared righteous in his sight by observing the law; rather, through the law we become conscious of sin. But now a righteousness from G-d, apart from law, has been made known, to which the Law and the Prophets testify."

I see it differently. Law, or precise rules of how we must live and behave, are central to religion. Judaism's earthward orientation, far from serving as an obstacle to spiritual exultation, is what grounds it in the real world. Our ritual ensures that we not only talk about values but practice them. We don't just talk about gratitude but say a blessing on every food we eat so that we never take even an apple for granted.

To us Jews, divine law constitutes the channels of communication—the most highly tuned frequency—through which people can come close to G-d. Values don't work unless they are part of the real world. The man who plows with the ox or sits stuck in rush-hour traffic is the same man who sits with a prayer book in synagogue. G-d does not wish to be thought of only in the synagogue. What kind of relationship would that be? A woman wants her husband to think of her even as he sits in the boardroom, not just the bedroom.

Religion has always faced accusations of hypocrisy. Religious people aren't always the most honest or the most compassionate, and throughout history religious people have been responsible for serious atrocities. That's why while other religions stand for lofty spiritual values, Jewish values are firmly grounded in the here and now. I have often heard it said that the G-d of the Old Testament is vengeful, whereas Jesus's teachings are more humane; that the Old Testament is about law, whereas the New Testament is about love. There are endless comparisons between the Hebrew Bible's "eye for an eye" (a law that the Rabbis have always interpreted to mean financial compensation rather than any barbaric extraction of an eye, which would be totally forbidden) and Jesus's magnanimous philosophy of "turn the other cheek." Surely this means that Jewish values don't exactly aid transcendence?

It is undeniable that Jewish values champion law above love, practice above faith, and religious service above theology and dogma. That's why Jewish values have been left so far behind. People prefer salvation to redemption. Salvation is an act of faith that is purchased in an instant. Redemption is a collective act of commitment that may take ages to acquire. And love feels a lot nicer than law. I agree.

But there is no love without law. Try having a relationship that has no rules. I have counseled many couples who live thus. I have counseled married couples who had an open relationship, wives who told their husbands they don't mind if they download hours of porn per night, husbands and wives who had no rules about how they spoke to each other. The outcome was never pretty. Would you live in a country with a ruler who professes love to his people but is not restrained by any law? Law is the channel through which love is shown and preserved. Jewish values dictate that love without law is nothing more than meaningless sentimentalism, which will ultimately end in cruelty. As the saying goes, "He who is kind to the cruel will end up being cruel to the kind."

A bright student once walked into my office holding a copy of Neale Donald Walsch's *Conversations with G-d*. "You just have to read this book," he said. "It's the most beautiful book about G-d." The book claims to be a direct prophetic dialogue with G-d and promotes the idea of feelings as absolutely central to religion. In the quest for G-d, the book says: "Ministers, Rabbis, Priests . . . even the Bible . . . are not authoritative sources. Then what is? Listen to your feelings. Listen to your highest thoughts. Listen to your experience. Whenever any of these differ from what you've been told by your teachers, or read in your books, forget the words. Words are the least reliable purveyor of Truth."

Walsch's book, an international best seller, spoke for a generation whose principal desire is to *feel* G-d rather than worship Him. Paul in his Epistles upbraided Judaism not just for privileging the law over a deeper kind of righteousness, but for an infatuation with words and codes. "For sin will have no dominion over you, since you are not under law but under grace," and again, "But now we are discharged from the law, dead to that which held us captive, so that we are slaves not under the old written code but in the new life of the Spirit."

In fact, the separation of law and religion has been a great calamity for human civilization. It means that atrocities can be perpetrated in the name of G-d and no one can say that religious law forbids it. That religion has lost out to secularism as the mainstream guide to life is a direct result of the detached role religion began to play when Christianity abrogated the law. If a misguided Muslim blows himself up on a bus because his religious heart tells him it's the best way to strike a blow for his faith, who is to tell him that what he has done is an abomination? Who is to tell him that these feelings were not from G-d but the devil? Surely only a religious law that says that killing in the name of G-d is abhorrent can do so.

To say that religion cannot be about law is to say that religion is not designed to regulate human life. The suggestion is that governments must step into the breach with legislation. Robbed of its G-d-given origin, law today is perceived as an unwelcome invader, rather than welcomed as a partner, in the lives of young men and women. It is something they either resent or try to outsmart.

But it is nonsense to say, as Walsch maintains, that G-d is found primarily in feelings. Why should we give our feelings free rein to govern our actions? Since when do feelings have any permanence? Would anyone go before a judge who declared that he adjudicates his cases on how he feels that day? Mark Sanford, the governor of South Carolina, was caught having an affair with an Argentinean woman. He told the press that his mistress was his real soul mate and he loved her rather than his wife. Sound convincing? Is he allowed to break the laws of his marriage because he feels like it? Is truth, and are relationships, really so capricious? If a man is angry at his son for failing to meet his expectations, does this justify not showing him affection? And what marriage could possibly survive on feelings alone, without action?

Judaism has always believed that actions, not feelings, are the surest way of determining the authenticity of love. Therefore, Judaism has always harbored an intense distrust of unguided emotions. Indeed, no marriage will ever succeed if a man can cheat on his wife and rationalize it by thinking that lately his wife has been distant and neglectful. The only way to preserve love is to preserve law.

Law has no expiration date or geographic constraints, and it is not subject to whim. It is operative at all times and in all places. In that light, the Ten Commandments are the perfect example of G-d's love for his creation. They set forth a moral code by which man is assured of relating to G-d, as well as his fellow man, with decency, justice, and affection.

Reflect for a moment on the Ten Commandments' utter simplicity. I once saw a poster in London that said, "Life . . . Come and hear one man make sense of it." It was an advertisement for a speech by Billy Graham. Now imagine that you are one of the 80,000 people who cram into Wembley Stadium to hear the famous preacher explicate the secret of life. The evangelist gets up and says, "Be nice to your mother. Also, I say it's a bad idea to steal. And adultery? Come on. Cheating on your wife is a sin." I assume you would be highly disappointed. *I waited in line for hours to hear this trite stuff?* You would feel ripped off. This stuff is obvious, right?

Imagine, then, how the Jews felt at Mount Sinai. For seven weeks they had spiritually prepared themselves for this great revelation. Moses had psyched them up. G-d Himself was to speak to them. And what did He say? Honor your father and your mother. Don't commit adultery. Don't be jealous of your friends. Don't covet your neighbor's wife. The Israelites' disappointment must have been enormous. One can imagine them asking, "For this we traveled fifty days in the desert?" The author and polemicist Christopher Hitchens put it this way: "However little one thinks of the Jewish tradition, it is surely insulting to the people of Moses to imagine that they had come this far under the impression that murder, adultery, theft, and perjury were permissible."

The importance of the Ten Commandments is not in their content—a human, and not even a very refined one, could have dictated these commandments—but in *that it was G-d who commanded them.* This concise code of conduct introduced immutable, divine law as the operating force in the universe. When mortals make laws, they become subject to human interpretation. They are easily manipulated and bargained away. Ronald Reagan once said, "I have wondered at times what the Ten Commandments would have looked like if Moses had run it through a state legislature." Humans have a knack for adapting laws to suit their own purposes and making them apply only to situations where it suits their fancy. When G-d gives commandments, however, they are universally applicable. The commandment not to steal is as relevant today as it was in ancient Mesopotamia, and as applicable here as it would be on Uranus or in an undiscovered galaxy.

What made the commandments so potent was not their content but their source. These were rules coming from G-d and therefore immutable. You can feel whatever you want, G-d was saying, but you still better not break my commandments. They are mine, not yours. So if you've fallen out of love with your wife and you're drawn to your secretary, I'm sorry. This doesn't give you one iota of license to cheat. Your feelings mean nothing in the face of my law. Get a divorce if you have to. But don't become a liar and do things behind your spouse's back.

It is notable that the Ten Commandments don't mention rewards or punishments. There are not even any rationalizations! G-d does not say, "Do not steal. After all, you would hate if it happened to you." G-d offers no possibility for argument or rebuttal. Rather, He simply says that these ten rules must be observed. Period. In all of ancient literature there is no other example of a code of conduct given so forcefully with no attempt even made to establish the credentials of the power making these demands. It is not because they make sense that the Ten Commandments are right and correct. They are law because G-d ordained them. End of discussion.

In Victor Hugo's classic *Les Misérables,* Jean Valjean, a poor man just released from prison with no prospects of earning money, steals a loaf of bread from a bakery to sustain his life. The proprietor of the bakery wishes to prosecute even though the loss incurred is minimal. Does the starving man deserve punishment? Has a crime been committed or not? If human conscience is the authority judging the validity of the act, then we could conclude that there was no transgression. Under the circumstances, the action of stealing the loaf of bread was justifiable, possibly even heroic. But stealing is forbidden by the Almighty, at all places and at all times. The poor man could have asked the bakery owner for the loaf. He could have worked for it. By stealing, he perhaps deprived himself of the opportunity to experience a fellow man's generosity.

But this is all beside the point. At Sinai we gave our assent to His commandments. We will abide by His will, even if we don't understand why.

The basis of every relationship between two parties is an accommodation of each other's needs. Each partner possesses an intrinsic will that is the deepest definition of his or her being. The very act of entering into a relationship is an undeclared, yet tacit, acceptance of the simple fact that no desire of one's beloved is trivial or irrelevant. Rather, if our beloved is dear to us, we will always seek to make that person happy, and this primarily involves accommodating the beloved's innermost will.

If a woman tells her husband she loves flowers, then he cannot buy her a box of chocolates instead, saying it's the thought that counts. Thus, the man or woman of faith who dismisses observance of Jewish law because some laws do not lend themselves to his or her rational apprehension is no different than a husband who refuses to buy his wife flowers because he cannot understand why she craves something that has no shelf life. Even his offer to buy her a ruby or emerald instead is still a rejection of her intrinsic womanhood. If she would only think like a man, if she would only crave items whose value does not diminish with time, then he would accommodate her.

Such a man is incapable of being in a relationship, because he can meet people only on his terms. Similarly, the man or woman of faith does not try to create G-d in his or her own image—or accept as binding only those religious practices he or she feels enrich human life—but rather accepts that G-d too has an intrinsic will that must be accommodated, irrespective of its immediate appreciation on the part of the human mind.

The idea of the G-d–man relationship mirroring that of husband and wife finds its strongest expression in kabbalistic writings. According to kabbalah, G-d, as mysterious as this may seem, has needs. G-d informs the Jewish people that He requires them to accommodate His will, such as refraining from desecrating the Sabbath, His holy day. The Creator also reveals that justice for Him is as great a passion as success is for man, so if you wish G-d to grant you success, you must always act justly.

Hence the first Jewish-values step in knowing G-d is to unconditionally accept His expressed will, though we may not understand it. G-d and man discover each other in accommodating the other's innermost desires. Real love in Jewish thought goes beyond attempting to make sense of each other; it involves an inner experience that translates externally into a desire to cater to the wishes of one's beloved.

This idea may seem unintelligible to men and women today who prize communication above accommodation. But those whose marriages last understand there can be nothing more romantic, and no better way to make someone feel cherished, than to respect, anticipate, and respond to the other person's needs and desires on a daily basis, and down to the details of everyday life. Similarly, according to both the spirit of the law and the law itself, the details of how G-d must be worshipped and the minutiae of the spiritual life are vitally important.

The ancient rabbis stated that the greatness of man, in contradistinction to his animal counterparts, is his ability to call G-d master, and accept the yoke of His will. If we were to forget G-d and abrogate our divinely mandated responsibilities, we would descend to the level of very clever animals. Our future would be too horrible to contemplate. The only thing protecting human dignity is the belief in an all-powerful Creator who will exact justice from those who destroy His creation.

Seen in this light, it comes as no surprise that the man who sought to abolish G-d and morality from the earth identified the Jews as his greatest enemies. Historians point out that Hitler's hatred of the Jews was so great that he even abandoned his soldiers, leaving them without food or ammunition, while the railroads continued to ferry Jews to the gas chambers. Hitler sought not only to win the war. *His principal objective was to establish a new set of values.* His biggest obstacle was the Jews: witnesses to G-d in history, the nation who gave the world the rule of divine law, and the guardians of the Ten Commandments.

Hitler said as much about the Jews and the carriers of their moral message, the Christians: "For the moment, I am just keeping my eye upon them: if I ever have the slightest suspicion that they are getting dangerous, I will shoot the lot of them. This filthy reptile raises its head whenever there is a sign of weakness in the State, and therefore it must be stamped on. We have no sort of use for a fairy story invented by the Jews."

But Judaism's insistence on immutable law as the sole guarantor of society's decency has further resonance when we consider science. What becomes of our standards once the belief that we are all children of the one G-d is jettisoned? Witness the similarity in these two statements:

"The more civilized so-called Caucasian races have beaten the Turkish hollow in the struggle for existence. Looking to the world at no very distant date, what an endless number of the lower races will have been eliminated by the higher civilized races throughout the world."

"In nature there is no pity for the lesser creatures when they are destroyed so that the fittest may survive. Going against nature brings ruin to man . . . and is a sin against the will of the eternal Creator. It is only Jewish impudence that demands that we overcome nature."

The first quotation comes from the letters of Charles Darwin. The second is from Hitler, who developed his concept of the Aryan master race according to what he saw as the ethical implications of evolutionary theory. Once man was robbed of the dignity of having been created in G-d's image and identified instead with evolutionary development from the ape, race theory—a belief that some human races are more highly developed than others—became inevitable. Hitler took the notion of the survival of the fittest in the animal kingdom and applied it to peoples and races.

Let me state emphatically that this does not in any way whatsoever make Darwin responsible for Hitler. And anyone who draws a direct connection between them is guilty of abhorrent defamation. But what this does demonstrate is how laws that are not rooted in a belief in the infinite value of every human being, or that don't acknowledge G-d as the source of those laws, can be horribly abused. Without the Ten Commandments, forbidding murder in any circumstance, people can even begin to believe that war is healthy for humanity since it eliminates the weak and rids the world of genetic waste, conferring upon the survivors important gifts.

It's dangerous to start thinking of humans in terms of race. I believe in ethnicity, not race. There is only one race, the *human* race. The danger of thinking otherwise, even when done by the most brilliant minds of our time, is illustrated by the comment made to the *New York Times* by James

Watson, the co-discoverer of DNA and one of the greatest scientists of the twentieth century, in relation to Africa. "[Watson]," the article said, is "inherently gloomy about the prospect of Africa" because, in his words, "all our social policies are based on the fact that their intelligence is the same as ours—whereas all the testing says not really, and I know that this 'hot potato' is going to be difficult to address." Such racist conclusions were common to the original evolutionists, such as Aldous Huxley, even as they have been abandoned by their successors.

The key in achieving a real appreciation of values is to understand that they are counterintuitive. We who have grown up in the Judeo-Christian tradition forget that values are not intrinsic or self-evident. And this is one of religion's foremost and most noble objectives. Murder and crime are normal, as we are assured by history. Values are abnormal and must be instilled. Only religion and the rule of divine law can safeguard humankind from the abyss.

Yet our desire to evade subjugation to divine law is both predictable and understandable. If we have a shallow understanding of freedom, we view G-d as the party pooper in chief. Scientist and philosopher Huxley, who came from a family of avid supporters of evolution theory, wrote at the end of his life:

> I had reasons not to want the world to have meaning, and as a result I assumed the world had no meaning, and I was readily able to find satisfactory grounds for this assumption. . . . For me, as it undoubtedly was for most of my generation, the philosophy of meaninglessness was an instrument of liberation from a certain moral system. We were opposed to morality because it interfered with our sexual freedom.

The goal of Jewish values is to empower man with real freedom, the freedom to bring out human goodness and liberate oneself from the cage of animal instinct. The man and woman who live with real values seek to create a loving and just society in which every person approaches the other with honesty, sincerity, and decency. This cannot be accomplished unless law is promoted above all else and unless morality is underpinned by immutable divine authority. Because many religious people have adopted a belief in G-d without a concomitant belief in law, countless religious atrocities have been perpetrated throughout history. The error of those who commit such evil is, as my friend Dennis Prager says, though they may believe in G-d, they do not believe that G-d's primary demand is moral behavior.

To the critics who argue that Jewish values are encumbered by too much law and too little emotion, my response is that we see law as the medium by which love is promoted, protected, and preserved. Where there is no law, there is no G-d. And where there is no G-d, there are no rules. And where there are no rules, there is no way to protect those who most need protection.

As the psalmist chanted, "I have always placed the Lord before me." Holiness is attained only when man forgoes the petty license that never brings true happiness, and instead opens his self to the possibility of G-d residing within.

CHAPTER 13

Leadership

It is amazing what you can accomplish if you do not care who gets the credit.

—HARRY S TRUMAN

I am absolutely convinced that no wealth in the world can help humanity forward, even in the hands of the most devoted worker. The example of great and pure individuals is the only thing that can lead us to noble thoughts and deeds.

—ALBERT EINSTEIN

An orchestra without a conductor will make noise, not music. Ever since the prophet Moses led the Hebrews from slavery in Egypt to the borders of Israel, leadership has been central to the Jewish nation. Indeed, there is a feeling among those who are conversant with the classic Jewish texts—the Torah, the Prophets, and the Talmud—that these giant leaders of Jewish history are in a sense alive even today. The Jews remain profoundly influenced not just by the teachings of Moses, but by his personality, charisma, humility, and integrity—all of which are timeless.

Why are leaders so important to the Jewish people? Can't social currents, as opposed to individuals, lead the way? It would certainly seem more desirable for society to give rise to righteousness of its own accord. Leadership, after all, has its drawbacks. It lends itself to tyranny and can foster dependence among the populace. Moses himself complained to G-d of this development: "Did I conceive this whole people? Did I give birth to them, that you should say to me, 'Carry them in your bosom, as a nurse carries a sucking child,' to the land that you promised on oath to their ancestors?" Yet Moses also prayed that the Jewish people would never be bereft of leadership: "Let the Lord, the G-d of the spirits of all flesh, appoint someone over the congregation, who shall go out before them and come in before them, who shall lead them out and bring them in, so that the congregation of the Lord may not be like sheep without a shepherd."

Leadership is central to Judaism because someone must serve as the living embodiment of G-dly teachings. A leader translates principles into practice, and idea into reality. A leader helps close the gap that normally exists between ideology and practical living. We hear the glorious stories of Abraham, who defended even the wicked habits of Sodom and Gomorrah when G-d sought to destroy them. We read that Moses was the most humble man who walked the earth. We read of Jewish masters throughout history, such as Don Isaac Abravanel, who chose to share the exile of his Jewish brethren in Portugal rather than lead a comfortable life in Spain as finance minister to Ferdinand and Isabella.

The primary purpose of every leader is to deprive us of our excuses. A leader challenges us to lead an inspired existence. The Talmud relates that when a poor man dies, his soul appears before the angels, who ask him whether he dedicated his life to G-d's will. The poor man answers, "Me, I couldn't. I was too poor. I had to struggle just to feed my family. There wasn't time for anything else." The angels then ask him, "Were you poorer than the great sage Hillel? Hillel was so poor that he had to climb in the snow to the rooftop of the study hall where Shemaya and Avtalyon were teaching, because he did not possess even the few coins it took to gain entry." To the rich man who complains that he had too many responsibilities to find time for such worthwhile pursuits as Torah study, the angels say, "Were you richer than the great Rabbi Eliezer ben Hyracanus, who owned a fleet of hundreds of vessels, and yet still found the time to become one of the great scholars of his generation?"

Personal examples make it impossible for us to maintain that the mountain's summit was too high for anyone to climb it.

The Bible goes out of its way to demonstrate the human qualities of its great heroes. Unlike the New Testament, which insists upon Christ's divinity, the people presented in the Jewish scriptures are human and fallible. Adam and Eve were misled by the serpent and sinned shortly after they were placed in Eden. Noah became drunk as soon as he emerged from the ark. Abraham erred in the rearing of Ishmael, and Isaac was misguided in cherishing Esau above Jacob. The Bible further relates that Jacob made the mistake of favoring his son Joseph over his other children. Even Moses was punished for the sin of hitting the rock to give forth water, rather than talking to it as G-d had commanded. David was led by lust to cavort with Bathsheba, and G-d punished him by allowing the first child of that union to die.

If heroes with such faults are capable of leading highly virtuous lives, then we are challenged to do the same. The problem, however, is that we tend to categorize these great men and women as saintly, removed from earthly reality. And the world much admires saints, but people rarely choose to emulate them. Raising individuals to the pedestal of sainthood is the perfect way to render them ineffective in shaping the lives of their followers. *Of course, Abraham was able to defy the entire pagan world! After all, he was a saint! But me? I'm just an ordinary person.* But by depicting all its heroes for what they were—ordinary people who led extraordinary lives—the Bible allows us to feel that we too can emulate their example.

The Jewish Messiah will not be a divine figure or the son of a deity, as in Christianity. Nor will he be a mystical angel who is immune to temptation. Rather, he will simply be someone who distinguishes himself by an ability to bring out the good in vast numbers of people.

Imagine for a moment a genius who, using the vast communication networks now at our disposal, spreads his message to the entire world. Now imagine that he is a true *tzaddik*—an individual whose righteousness is recognized by all. It may once have seemed impossible for a holy man to assume a role in world leadership, but the world is becoming more accustomed to accepting leaders of all races, religions, and ethnic groups. Think of the vast respect accorded to such men as Pope John Paul II, Nelson Mandela, and the Dalai Lama. Indeed, today the opinions of numerous religious leaders are sought by political leaders on all issues. It is not farfetched to picture a great man, or rabbi, in such a role.

Some believe that awaiting a leader to spur us on to these efforts is misguided. They believe that rather than an identifiable historical figure, the collective efforts of humanity all represent the Messiah. But Judaism never conceived of a Jesus-like figure who would come along and redeem mankind of its iniquity irrespective of its actions. That would be utterly disempowering. Spiritual dependency is not the purpose of messianism. On the contrary. The Messiah will not act magisterially and undertake people's responsibilities for them. The Messiah will be a leader who will inspire people to redeem themselves. He will stimulate action and transformation. He will orchestrate human effort into a coherent whole that will create the conditions necessary to usher in redemption.

In a word, rather than making followers, the Messiah is a leader who will inspire others to become leaders as well.

The Messiah represents the ability of all of us to find our fullness, destiny, and redemption. Into a world that has become disillusioned about the future and is concerned with self-preservation and prosperity will come a comforting redeemer who will renew human belief in the possibility of creating a majestic world built on the twin foundations of love and justice.

Here we come to the most important aspect of messianism: Each of us has a portion in the world only we can redeem. To the young child waiting at home for his father to return from work, that man is a Messiah. He may not be able to redeem the entire world, but he can redeem the tiny world that is his son. He is who plays with the child and makes him feel loved. No one else can take his place. To a man broken by the pain of the world, his wife is a Messiah. She comforts him and makes him feel indispensable, even when his employers have just fired him or when he finds himself racked with illness. To the woman who has always dreamed of finding love, the man who comes home to her every night and tells her she is the most special person on the planet is a Messiah, redeeming her from ordinariness and constant comparison with other women. To the friend whose relationship has just broken up and who desperately seeks someone to talk to, you are a Messiah. Nobody else can take your place. If you can't find the time to talk to your friend, you will leave that part of the world in an unredeemed state.

Every American child believes he can grow up to be president. Every Jewish child should grow up believing that he could be the Messiah. He will then exert every effort to improve himself and his surroundings. If we each believe that we could be the Messiah, then we will never pass up an opportunity to feed the hungry, comfort the bereaved, uplift the helpless, and inspire the young. Nine hundred years ago, Maimonides wrote that every individual has the capacity to redeem the whole world. He wrote that one must always see the world as being perfectly balanced between good and evil. If a single individual does even one good deed, that tips the earth's balance into righteousness and redemption. But be careful, for the opposite is true as well. A single evil deed can make everyone else guilty.

Historically, messianic pretensions have been the scourge of the Jewish people. The rejection of the messiahship of Jesus has led to millions of

Jewish deaths throughout the ages. Likewise, embracing false such messiahs as Shabbatai Zevi, the seventeenth-century messianic pretender from Turkey, led to global Jewish disillusionment. Thousands of Jews sold their properties in anticipation of the final redemption before discovering that the man in whom they had placed all their hopes had converted to Islam. In the fifth century, Moses of Crete, promising the Jews that the millennium was at hand, encouraged his followers to jump into the sea, which he promised to part. Hundreds drowned.

These calamities came about when one person claimed to be the Messiah. The most dangerous human is the one who claims to have all the answers but has no proof of any divine appointment. What we need are millions of Messiahs, working in unison, to bring about the final redemption. Every doctor who saves a life is a Messiah. Every man who loves a woman and makes her feel cherished is a Messiah. Every businessman who feeds the poor is a Messiah. Every individual who prays for a loved one's recovery from illness is a Messiah. Every cleric who brings his congregants closer to G-d is a Messiah. And every child who shares his toys with another child is a Messiah.

The contribution of these millions of Messiahs and the cumulative effect of their efforts will one day produce the individual who will encourage the earth's inhabitants to deliver the final push.

In November 2009 I and my friend Dennis Prager traveled to Zimbabwe as guests of an outstanding Christian organization, Rock of Africa. We visited an orphanage in Harare, the capital of Zimbabwe, that housed sixteen children whose parents had died of AIDS. When we arrived, the children sang to us and danced. They were immaculately attired and even better behaved. Even in one of the poorest countries on earth, these children were happy and well looked after. It quickly became apparent that the four women who ran the orphanage were the reason for the children's incredible balance. They held the children tightly and made them feel loved. They were the children's deliverers. They redeemed these beautiful young lives.

So why do we need the Almighty to send a single individual to lead us out of the morass, rather than rely on the efforts of a united humanity? Because even as man endeavors to end pain, he is haunted by the fact that personal considerations often fuel social advance. The doctor who will one day cure AIDS labors strenuously not only out of a love for mankind, but also because he craves a Nobel Prize. The CEO who builds libraries insists that his name be chiseled over the front door. One can never fully separate oneself from narcissism and personal interest.

Only G-d can lend the spark that will allow us humans to transcend self-interest. Therefore, only G-d's chosen redeemer can liberate us from human shortcomings. One of the Messiah's most important functions will be to teach us how to do right because it is right. Only then will we enjoy righteous action inspired by altruistic motivation. By so doing, the Messiah will bring about perfection of the world at large and the inner world of man, simultaneously.

CHAPTER 14

Redirection

∞∞∞∞∞∞∞∞∞∞

Prayer does not change God, but it changes him who prays.

—SØREN KIERKEGAARD

What men usually ask of God when they pray is that two and two not make four.

—ANONYMOUS

As a young boy, I often witnessed my parents arguing. I remember feeling lonely. But it was also at this age that I started concentrating on the words of my daily prayers. They comforted me. When I prayed I felt that G-d was near me. "He heals the brokenhearted and binds up their wounds." I felt that He would never abandon me. I would never be alone.

Now I am a rabbi with a family of my own. Sadly, prayer is not the same companion it once was. Awash in responsibilities, I often go about my daily prayers in a rush. My manner is often like that of a person trying to discharge an obligation. Rather than enjoying the journey, I race to the finish line.

However unintentional, this is a deep denial of prayer's extraordinary force. Imagine a man who lives in a dingy basement apartment in a bad neighborhood in Queens. As he trudges home after his late-night shift restocking grocery store shelves, he is regularly harassed by thugs. He has been mugged several times for the measly handful of cash he takes home every day. The thugs don't fear the police because, as they suspect, the man is an illegal alien and so won't report the crime. Then one day they watch in awe as the man is picked up by motorcade and taken to lunch at the Four Seasons, where New York Mayor Michael Bloomberg listens intently to his cries for protection and relief.

This story illustrates what prayer is all about. What a gift that the Creator of heaven and earth suspends His affairs and listens to the distressed cry of one of his children. It lends us an incomparable dignity. In *Who Is Man?* Abraham Joshua Heschel writes, "Dark for me is the world for all its bright cities and shiny stars, if not for the knowledge that G-d listens to me when I cry." And without G-d listening, who could maintain hope in a world with so much suffering?

Our generation has little understanding of, or appreciation for, the deeply emotional prayer. This is partly because we have lost an admiration for the power of words. In Judaism, words are of surpassing importance. The Bible relates how G-d created the world with words: "He said, 'Let there be light,' and there was light." Even in everyday situations, we use words to create other people. Give someone a compliment, offer her a kind word when she is feeling low, and watch her come to life. A man who works at a sewing machine churning out hundreds of garments per month feels ignored and angry until his boss comes by one day to thank him and commend him for doing an excellent job. At the same time, one abusive and angry word can make us feel existentially threatened.

Why do words have such power? Because they are the pathways of the spirit, the pipeline through which all sentiment must pass. The words

I use in conversation are a reflection, an effusion, of my deepest essence. But they not only reflect the condition of my own soul, they also have the capacity to shape another. And words of prayer are the very bricks that build the bridge between G-d and man.

In its purest sense, Jewish prayer is an acknowledgment that G-d alone can provide comfort and redemption. It refutes the indifferent G-d of the deists who say that G-d created the world, then left it to its own devices.

A friend whose marriage was crumbling told me he had done everything to keep it together, from going to marriage counselors to taking his wife away on a safari, all to no avail. "Nothing has worked," he told me, "and I am now ready to give up." "Have you tried praying?" I asked him. "If you could open your heart to G-d in prayer, you may also prove capable of opening your heart to your wife's needs." When humans call out to G-d to provide sustenance for themselves and their families, they acknowledge G-d as a force with a direct impact on the material world.

On one level, prayer is about asking G-d for our daily wants. But prayer's supreme purpose is to recalibrate our desires. If we had a child who was sick, in the hospital, would we pray to G-d for a larger house? The history of humankind is one of mistaken priorities and muddled values. When we listen to the words of the prayers and open our hearts to their power, we focus on life's purpose. When a man prays daily for the health of his children, he is reminded of how much more important they are than spending more time at the office.

Prayer is a fundamental redirection. Heschel said that by praying we effectively proclaim, *Let there be more G-d in this world. Let us cause all the earth to recognize His name. Let His glory illuminate the dark corners of the earth and the dingy alleys of the mind.* Prayer is like a chorus of bells going off in the mind, alerting us to the human mission and obliterating false illusions.

Jewish prayer is recited in Hebrew. The text comes from the Siddur, the Jewish prayer book, which includes psalms and an order of blessings arranged by the men of the Great Assembly more than 2,000 years ago.

Many have complained, however, that the rigidity of a set prayer book is stultifying and impedes individual feeling. They object to having to pray in a foreign language, and they protest at having a fixed text composed of words that were written ages ago. My students tell me they would rather take a banjo out into the fields and "sing a new song to the Lord" that is both personal and spontaneous. They feel stultified in having to pray from a prepared text.

These objections miss a crucial point. The great secret of Jewish prayer is that it is not about talking, but listening. It is about imbibing G-d. We awaken in the morning and pray not so much to praise Him as to listen to the beautiful words that remind us of how He is all about us. The words of the prayer book are like a chisel that slowly carves away our stony edges and fashions us into divine beings. These words tenderize our hearts so that we may serve the one true G-d. Jewish prayer is an art where we remain silent and allow ancient words to ignite our soul and fashion our heart. As others have noted, the Jewish prayers are like walking through an art gallery and being inspired by timeless masterpieces.

In the course of counseling people I have noticed that many people prefer to say their own prayers. But the curse of our generation is that we don't even know what to wish for. By the time people in crisis come to me, finding a way to achieve their dreams isn't even discussed. Our first task is to correct the dreams they identified in the first place.

One man asked me to save his marriage. His wife had already forced him to move out because, as she said, he was never home anyway. She refused the illusion of marriage with a man who never wanted to be with her. "I love her, I really do. But my thinking was I should spend the first years of our marriage working hard and building my business. I had to go to endless client dinners. My plan always was to establish financial security and then really enjoy my wife and kids." Here was a man who prayed for, and received, financial security. He had no idea that real security comes from having a wife who loves you and waits for you to come home at night. The famous saying "Be careful what you wish for" applies even more so to prayer. Be careful what you pray for.

In praying daily from a text that lists all that is valuable in life, we are reminded of what is truly worth prizing. We are redirected away from false gods. I've been praying from a Jewish prayer book my whole life. Let's see. Without it, I guess this is what I would pray for every day:

1. Lord, please make me successful in my public life. Let my books sell, let my TV appearances be popular, and let me be much in demand on the lecture circuit.
2. Let me find favor in the eyes of those who meet me, and let me be popular and liked.
3. Please ensure, G-d, that I always have money to support my family.
4. And thinking of my beautiful family, Lord, please always take care of them. Please protect my wife and children always.

But the Jewish prayer book gives me different goals. I am put at the back. What the psalms and other prayers have me emphasize every morning is:

1. Please, Lord, let me find favor in Your eyes by doing Your will.
2. Allow me to see the awe and wonder in daily creation, and how nothing is ordinary. Let me see how my wife and children are Your miracles, oh Lord, so that I never take them for granted.
3. Lead me to a life of righteousness and good deeds, Lord, where my success is employed in the pursuit of loftier goals.
4. Walk with me always, Lord, and never let me be alone.

Notice that in the Jewish prayers G-d is no longer the means to my ends; I am the means to His.

This is not to say that there are not moments when we can and should offer our own personal prayer. The Jewish values perspective on prayer is that there are two forms of prayer, the empathetic and the inspirational. Empathetic prayer is designed to create a spiritual ambience. It is carried out even when a person may not be in the mood to pray. You awaken in the morning, eager to get on with the urgent. But you suspend your many responsibilities as you take time out to pray. You concentrate on the meaning of the words, and as you do so, the words begin to touch you. You absorb their power. You empathize with their meaning. They awaken within you a desire to draw nearer to G-d and to be a better person. You want your day to have purpose. As you experience even a faint hint of G-d in your life, your compassion toward others is awakened and some of your selfishness is kept at bay. "Bestow peace, goodness and blessing, life, graciousness, kindness and mercy, upon us and upon all Your people Israel."

But there is a second kind of prayer, a little more personal and a little more spontaneous. This inspirational prayer occurs when you are moved to offer thanks to G-d for the blessings that surround you and the wonders of creation. I experienced this kind of prayer on an airplane back from Africa to the United States. On the nonstop flight of nearly seventeen hours, I was pondering all I had seen in Zimbabwe and Zambia as a volunteer for the Christian relief organization I mentioned in Chapter 13. The breathtaking poverty in the mud-hut villages, the endless beautiful faces of tiny orphans whose parents were stolen by HIV. The political oppression and death squads of Robert Mugabe. Suddenly I sat up in my airplane chair, looked upward, and said, "Lord, thank you for the health of my children. Thank you for the peace you grant us in the land in which we live. And more than anything else, thank you for the blessing of a wife. Without her I would feel an incalculable loneliness. Please protect them all, Lord, and may we always be deserving of your Presence." The prayer was stirred from the depths of my soul. Everyone around me was sleeping. But I could think of little else.

This kind of inspiration should come to us all the time. Surely we all have experienced moments in which the miracle of creation so overtakes us that we feel the need to offer homage to "He who spoke and brought the world into being." One sees a beautiful sunset and is suddenly moved to praise G-d. One witnesses a relative recovering from illness and is moved to offer thanks to the fountainhead of life. We bite into a fresh peach and give thanks to G-d for our five senses.

Although inspirational prayer is important, the rule should be prayer as empathy, where we come to be educated by the process of prayer. In empathetic prayer, we open our hearts to G-d, making ourselves into receptacles for His blessing. Rather than our trying to tell G-d how much our heart swells with joy and thanksgiving, we give G-d Himself the opportunity to tell us what He is. Inspirational prayer allows us to discover G-d in certain places and at certain highly charged moments. Empathetic prayer teaches us to uncover the hidden G-d in all places and at all moments.

CHAPTER 15

Smashing Idols

ᴑᴑᴑᴑᴑᴑᴑᴑᴑᴑᴑᴑᴑ

I have not loved the world, nor the world me;
I have not flattered its rank breath, nor bowed
To its idolatries a patient knee,
Nor coined my cheek to smiles, nor cried aloud
In worship of an echo.

—LORD BYRON

Idolatry is really not good for anyone. Not even
the idols.

—JOHN BACH

I dolatry sounds rather old-fashioned. We don't think of idolatry much these days. We think about it about as often as we think of corsets, the cotton gin, steamboats, and the potter's fields of Victorian England—which is to say, not often at all. We think we've put idolatry safely behind us.

How did we become so confident that we had licked this one? I believe this confidence is based on the mistaken idea that idolatry entails prostrating oneself before stone, a mountain range, or a golden calf. Thus it would appear that the Bible's incessant attempts to pull people away from idolatry has little contemporary relevance. But the real definition of idolatry is simply living for something other than G-d, devoting your life to a goal other than righteousness and goodness. Idolatry means not only worshipping idols but also elevating something human or material to the status of a sacred object.

G-d demands not just our faith but all of us. As Moses discovered at the burning bush, the G-d of Israel is a consuming fire. A passion for materialism cannot coexist with our passion for G-d. The two are mutually exclusive. A love of money snuffs out our G-dly fire. G-d and idols cannot sit side by side. One has to give.

But there are other, even more insidious forms of contemporary idolatry. Hard-core astrology—the belief that such forces as stars and constellations control our destiny—is certainly idolatry, as is any belief in a predetermined fate, as we discussed in Chapter 1. Our future is determined not by fate or stars but by the morality of our actions.

Idolatry can also mean fearing another person more than we fear G-d. It includes elevating a political cause over the exercise of morality. For example, it is idolatrous to believe that the Land of Israel is holy for any reason other than G-d's proximity to it. The Bible declares explicitly that the holiness of Israel, to which the Jews are so irrevocably attached, is entirely because this is "a land which the Lord, your G-d, cares for; the eyes of the Lord your G-d are upon it, from the beginning of the year to the end of the year." It possesses no intrinsic holiness. G-d's presence makes it holy.

Indeed, patriotism and nationalism, when divorced from ethical conduct, are classic forms of idolatry. All idolatry arises from the hubris of creating G-d in our own image rather than remembering that we are created in His.

But we also become idolatrous when we grant the ephemeral precedence over the eternal. G-d is meant to be the focus of our existence, around which all else revolves. The sum total of our thoughts, actions, and speech—the money we make and the relationships we create—should lead us to a more sublime, higher purpose, making us more spiritual and sensitive human beings. Idolatry replaces that focus with something else, whether it be the pursuit of money, sex, art, education, celebrity, or even religion.

I thought I'd catch your attention with that last point. Yes, religions can also become idols. And very easily. Many people are so much more interested in promoting their religion than in being close to G-d. Their faith has become the object of their worship rather than G-d, who is supposed to be the center of the Faith. A suicide bomber who will kill because he thinks the West has insulted Islam has deified Islam. He does not care at all what G-d wants. G-d makes it clear he doesn't want people to murder. Not in His name, not in their own name, and not in Islam's name. But this cold-blooded killer has no interest in G-d. He never thinks of G-d. He has contempt for G-d. He worships Islam. And he will promote Islam even if it flies in the face of G-d's will.

Or take some of my Christian brothers and sisters who mistakenly preach that Jews who do not believe in Jesus are going to hell. Whose interest does this preaching promote—G-d's or Christianity's? Sure sounds pretty exclusive to me. Shouldn't they instead be preaching that G-d is the goal of every faith, and as long as people live a G-dly, righteous life, even within the context of a different faith, they are all going to heaven?

My Jewish brothers and sisters are likewise not immune to the deification of faith. Some believe that being a good Jew comes before being a good person. So people who would never eat non-kosher food or work on the Sabbath can find themselves being less than honest in their business dealings. A man who would never miss even one of the thrice-daily prayers but then cheats on his wife has not only betrayed his marriage, he has betrayed G-d and made a mockery of his religion. For he has shown that it is his Jewish faith that matters more to him than the G-d who commanded all the *mitzvot* in the Jewish faith and is surely heartbroken when

He witnesses a man destroying his wife's self-esteem for his own selfish interests.

Seen in this light, we can appreciate why idolatry is the most serious sin in the Bible. If a person has character flaws—a bad temper or an inability to be charitable—we can say he is basically a good person but that an element of his personality needs refinement. Idolatry, however, means that one's entire life is a sham. *What's at your very core is fraudulent.* Your fundamental existence is fundamentally off. When one practices idolatry, or lives entirely for money or status, one hasn't veered off the main road into a temporary tributary. No, such a man is headed in the wrong direction completely and will never end up in a good place.

An individual may sacrifice to his man-made G-d, pray to it, and worship it with all his heart and soul. But if it is a false G-d, then he is not merely committing an error, he has dedicated his life to something utterly pointless. In the modern age, many of us make the mistake of living for materialistic pursuits—cars that break down, homes that slowly deteriorate, sexual relationships that leave us feeling empty, academic degrees that, if not employed to a higher cause, lead to arrogance and vanity. This is why Maimonides says all the commandments ultimately are designed to wean us away from idolatry. Life is too precious a commodity to squander.

A realization first hit me in my twenty-second year when I began to assume the full responsibilities of a communal and university rabbi at Oxford. Like so many of my colleagues, I lectured my students on the beauty of Jewish life and Jewish tradition and how we could not allow ourselves to be the generation that severed the link with our ancestors' faith. But an alarm should have gone off. Was I beginning to speak of religion as if it were an end in itself, as if the preservation of tradition and an adherence to Jewish law were the ultimate purpose of the Jew, instead of religion being the means by which man created a loving relationship with G-d?

Many consider the story of the binding of Isaac, what we Jews call the *Akeida,* to be the Bible's most troubling story. What was G-d doing in commanding Abraham to murder his own son? My teacher, Rabbi Menachem Schneerson, the Lubavitcher Rebbe, offers the illuminating insight that Isaac represented not just an individual person, but rather Judaism as a whole. The monotheistic faith that Abraham had fathered would continue only through Isaac, as Ishmael had already left the fold. If Isaac died, Judaism would die with him. In essence, the test G-d presented to Abraham was to choose between his G-d and his religion. Which would Abraham put first, his relationship with G-d or his personal faith?

Would Abraham make the same mistake of today's fundamentalists who are more interested in promoting their faith than they are in G-d? Would Abraham destroy the faith he fathered if G-d commanded him to do so? Abraham passed the test, and both he and his son survived to establish G-d, for all ages to come, as master of the universe and centerpiece of religious devotion.

Religious fundamentalism is the contemporary world's most dangerous idol, supplanting G-d with religion itself. Contrary to popular belief, fundamentalists are not G-d-intoxicated. Rather, they are almost totally bereft of G-d, having replaced Him with the worship of ritual and the deification of religion. In reality, they are intoxicated with themselves. They have no relationship with G-d. Religious fundamentalists have far more in common with extreme nationalists than with G-d worshippers. One worships his country, the other worships his religion. Both have created false idols. The religious fundamentalist is as distant from G-d as the world's staunchest atheist.

None of the major religions is immune from fundamentalism. The truly evil incidents of Islamic suicide bombers or Christian extremists who assassinate abortion doctors are a troubling example of worshipping faith at the expense of G-d. Even in Judaism I see many people who are immediately judgmental of the less religious people who surround them. Their religious faith does not make them humble, it makes them arrogant and dismissive of those who are different. Religious fundamentalists actually get riled, to the point of violence, when people embrace G-d in a way of which they don't approve. We should stop calling terror organizations such as Al Qaeda and Hamas religious extremists. Rather, we should refer to them for what they are: worshippers of their own petty prejudice. These people are pious frauds.

The religious man is one whose heart is open to all his fellow beings. As the ancient rabbis proclaimed: "Who is wise? He who learns from everyone." Those who love and worship G-d are happy for people to embrace Him in a way that may differ from their own. They are focused not on the means but on the end. Their main priority is that G-d become central to people's lives.

As we move closer to G-d, we experience our own insignificance in the face of divine perfection. Conceit and proximity to G-d are inversely proportional. The arrogant man, the know-it-all, for whom life is a destination rather than a journey, is like a full cup into which no spirituality can be poured. As Rabbi Israel Baal Shem Tov said, "There is no room for G-d in a person who is full of himself." Values-based lives are designed to smash the idols of the self so we can truly and fully experience the divine.

CHAPTER 16

Rejecting Judgmentalism

∞∞∞∞∞∞∞∞∞∞

Behind everyone who behaves as if he were superior to others, we can suspect a feeling of inferiority which calls for very special efforts of concealment. It is as if a man feared that he was too small and walked on his toes to make himself seem tall.

—ALFRED ADLER

Be curious, not judgmental.

—WALT WHITMAN

I must confess a personal loathing. Judgmental people really rub me the wrong way. Few realize it's their own inner brokenness that compels them to put others down to feel good about themselves.

Many of my Jewish brothers and sisters who return to their Jewish roots and become observant suddenly feel the need to dismiss what they see as the selfish and materialistic lifestyles of those who surround them and are not as religious. The Christian Right spends much of its time condemning the loose mores and lifestyles of the general population, and especially Hollywood and the political Left. While there is certainly truth to the accusation that much of American culture is corrosive, shallow, and exploitative, it does not change the fact that condemnation is no substitute for inspiration. We do not choose a values-based life because we wish to reject our past. We choose values in order to improve our present. Humility resides at the core of a values-based life, and judgment and humility are in fundamental conflict.

And yes, I get it. I too criticize our society's slack listlessness. But such pronouncement cannot come from a spirit of judgment. It has to come from a spirit of promise, of wanting to lift people up rather than condemn them to make ourselves artificially feel better. I still remember how right after 9/11 we witnessed the lamentable spectacle of two leading Christian clergymen saying the attacks happened because G-d had removed his protection from an increasingly sinful nation. Come on. Is that how you impart values? By warning people that if they don't change they're going to die violently?

I am not going to defend what I, too, see as an increasingly base popular culture. But the implication that American sin caused September 11 is an abomination. I strongly object to the belief that being critical is the first calling of a values-based life, as if those who do not share our values are degenerate. I have spent my life trying to get people, myself included, to prioritize what's important. That does not change the fact that those who claim to live by proper values, yet have no humility, in truth have no values either.

Embracing G-d should involve enhancing the light rather than condemning the darkness. The truly spiritual person finds it difficult to dismiss any person, place, or thing, because he perceives G-d to lie wherever his eyes roam. Why do I contend that judgmentalism is the very antithesis of the values-based experience? Because the whole purpose of values is to provide a means by which the individual can live a meaningful life. And the closer one draws to the most meaningful things, the more awed one becomes with G-d's perfection and our own imperfection. One becomes more, not less, meek.

When I began my rabbinical studies at age fourteen, I quickly found myself lost amid the myriad details of a truly vast religion. I went in despair to the head of my yeshiva, an elderly sage, and asked him to sum up Judaism for me in a single axiom. He held my shoulders lovingly as if I were his only son and said, "The essence of Judaism is this: Take G-d very seriously and never take yourself seriously."

One cannot raise oneself above the everyday affairs of life unless one focuses on one's responsibility to be sensitive to G-d's will and to make oneself secondary to it. But we cannot compromise our humanity in the process. I have met too many religious people who spout religious rhetoric as if they were a tape recorder. They don't think about what they're saying and they've never really absorbed it. They are boring. Worst of all, they are conformists, parroting religious truths to fit into a group rather than because they really believe.

G-d does not want us in the course of fulfilling His will to cease feeling the beautiful human traits of compassion, joy, mercy, tolerance, fraternity, gratitude, and empathy. Nor does he want us to cease being individuals. Religious people who follow the herd are sad people who will never know truth because they have a personal relationship with the mob rather than with G-d. A values-based life elevates and enhances us. It is not meant to repress or suppress our basic human desires, but rather redirect them toward higher ends.

The judgmental person fails here. He has no humility because he begins to think he is closer to G-d than is everyone else. In his mind he becomes synonymous with G-d. His will is G-d's will, his desires G-d's desires. Here we have the most dangerous facet of religious extremism. The extremist talks himself into believing that whatever he feels or does is sanctioned by G-d. To be sure, in his warped mind he sees himself as an obedient servant subordinated to G-d's will. But the disdain he feels for G-d's children betrays his arrogance. Yigal Amir decided that Yitzhak

Rabin was a traitor who deserved death. Instead of thinking to himself, "Who am I? Even if I think this, I am not G-d, and my opinion is of no real significance," he decided that becoming judge and executioner would meet with favor in his G-d's eyes. Osama bin Laden decided that he alone understood G-d's true will, even though that understanding directly contradicted everything G-d said in every religion that claims to speak in his name.

In all these cases, religious belief led to unfathomable levels of arrogance that resulted in unspeakable tragedy. When the believer can no longer distinguish between himself and G-d and thinks that because he is religious, he is closer to G-d than those who are unlike him, then no form of cruelty is beyond him. He has granted himself the divine license to destroy life. Judgmentalism is ugly and lethal.

The judgmental person fails in developing a human self as well, since he suppresses his natural empathy for his fellow man in the misguided belief that G-d would have wished him to do so. He dismisses his humanity in the corrupt belief that it hinders him from carrying out a divine imperative. Here we come to the second most dangerous facet of religious extremism: A human being becomes a dangerous fanatic whenever he concludes that his humanity is incompatible with his religion, or that his empathy is an impediment to faith.

G-d does not want us to suppress our humanity, but rather to cultivate our goodness and holiness by channeling our actions to works of public and private utility. In Judaism, the deity has no earthly manifestation, and no man could ever proclaim himself to be G-d. To do so would be the ultimate act of heresy. The most important value is the recognition that G-d is the source of all values. They're not yours. Stop believing so much in yourself. They didn't stem from your brain but from G-d's will. So be humble. G-d is above you. Don't become your own creator.

The ancient rabbis declared that G-d originally sought to create the world with strict justice. After all, justice is the guardian of truth. But G-d saw that the earth could not endure that way. People are imperfect.

Humanity is frail. He therefore mixed into the world's foundation a healthy balance of love and compassion. The rabbis compared G-d to a king who, in order to prevent a fragile goblet from shattering, must mix hot and cold water when filling it. Justice must be mixed with mercy for the world to function. Even G-d's justice is often tempered by His mercy: "My heart recoils within me, My compassion grows warm and tender. I will not execute My fierce anger, I will not again destroy Ephraim; for I am G-d and not man."

The Bible recognizes that justice is never enough. The bridge between G-d and man is grace. Love is G-d's most supreme attribute, so most Jewish prayers are geared toward appealing to G-d's kindness. We supplicate G-d to be mindful of His love for us, even when we may not be deserving. We ought to extend the same gift toward our fellow man.

CHAPTER 17

Repentance

∘∘∘∘∘∘∘∘∘∘∘∘∘∘∘

Innocence is like polished armor; it adorns and defends.
—BISHOP ROBERT SOUTH

A clear and innocent conscience fears nothing.
—ELIZABETH I

Each of us has regrets. We may have behaved impulsively. We may have embarked upon a course of action that did not accord with our truest self. We may allow our passions to make decisions for us and wind up at a destination radically different from what we first envisaged. We may eventually start to feel that the mistakes we've made will haunt us forever. I've even met young, robust people in their twenties and thirties who feel it is too late to start afresh. You can imagine how much more painful this feeling is to people who are advanced in age, with less room and time to maneuver.

Jewish values completely reject this kind of thinking. We believe that actions are supremely important but not, in the final analysis, what define us as people. In the same way that possessions do not define our innate worth—rich and poor alike—so too the errors we commit do not penetrate our spirit. Both the righteous and the sinner are loved by their Creator, the only exception being the truly wicked who live to inflict cruelty on the innocent and who have snuffed out the spirit of G-d from within.

There is always a layer of innocence and purity that hides beneath our actions. Although they may corrupt us, these actions cannot ultimately corrupt our spirit. It is always possible to start afresh by tapping into this layer of holiness, the soft virgin snow that lies just underneath our coarse exterior. Deep within our character there is a shining G-dly component that remains impervious to human caprice and whim. It is not destroyed by death nor is its light diminished by sin. We can always find it, tap into it, and reclaim our innocence.

Yom Kippur is the holiest and most solemn day of the Jewish calendar because it is devoted to summoning forth this quintessential spark, the deepest part of ourselves. During this great celestial bath, twenty-five hours of fasting and prayers, the sins of the nation and the individual are washed away and a pristine and sparkling person without taint or blemish emerges. Yom Kippur comes as the culmination of ten days of repentance, which begin with the two days of Rosh Hashanah, the Jewish New Year. It commemorates Moses's second ascension of Mount Sinai to beg G-d to forgive the Jews for their sin of building the golden calf. The enterprise took forty more days, and on the final day, G-d proclaimed, "I have forgiven them as you have requested." We use Yom Kippur's immense power to renew our commitment to righteousness. The Hebrew word for repentance, *teshuvah*, literally means "return." Repentance is a return to the path of honor, but more important, a return to our truest selves.

Every person, Jewish or not, requires a day of atonement, a day to experience the life-affirming quality of being utterly purged of mistakes. Everyone needs to know that the mistakes we made will not be carried with us. We can move forward without that baggage. Every year we can start life anew, unencumbered by the past, and with the promise of our destiny in front of us.

Legendary baseball pitcher Sandy Koufax refused to pitch in the World Series on Yom Kippur, and even Wall Street virtually ceases to function on this day. Even now, when many Jews are not religiously observant, about 90 percent still go to synagogue on Yom Kippur. For many it constitutes their only annual Jewish observance. Even people who are secular naturally understand the importance of no longer feeling haunted by our ghosts.

The ancient rabbis point out that G-d treats each of our transgressions as if it is being committed for the first time, irrespective of how often the action occurred. There is no such thing as a permanent record. Our plea for forgiveness is treated as though we are beseeching Him for the first time. No residue or grudge builds up. The human belief that we cannot undo our bad behavior has no basis in spiritual reality.

What would happen if we thought our mistakes would always come back to haunt us? Our extremely judgmental world relishes reminding people of their mistakes whenever they contemplate public office or try to undertake the common good. From the perspective of Jewish values, such actions would be immoral. Maimonides lists as law that a person should never remind a friend of something bad they did once they have changed their ways. It is as if the sin was committed by another man. The new person before us cannot be found guilty of something his former self did. Once a man has steered his life away from sinful ways, it is unlawful to remind him of his errors. Indeed, the ancient rabbis taught that a penitent is a totally new person. Not only is it improper to remind him of his former ways, *it is also inaccurate.* The sinful man you speak of no longer exists.

Repentance gives us the opportunity to reestablish our relationship with the Creator. We get used to thinking that all we really require to survive are food, clothing, and shelter. But our spirit has minimum requirements as well. I am convinced that nothing is more essential for sustaining the soul's well-being than innocence. Corruption leads to insanity. We cannot live with a self that has been fundamentally weakened by continual error. We begin to loathe our existence, taking little pride in whom we have become.

Corruption leads to an inner compartmentalization between the person we wish to be and the person we've actually become. The two divided parts are at war with each other, robbing us of inner peace. Notice how truly selfish people never evince an inner restfulness. They are fidgety and edgy. They are always on the move to satisfy a voracious desire for more and more pleasure. The inner cavity they seek to fill has been hollowed out of the self, creating a chasm born of the loss of peacefulness and innocence.

But the soul shines when it feels blameless, and the necessity of innocence by far transcends the needs of the soul alone. Indeed, returning to our innocence is essential to our mental, physiological, and ultimately physical well-being.

Strife occurs when we feel as if we are being pulled apart from the inside, when our actions no longer reflect our convictions. If a person feels fragmented, she cannot approach her life with any sense of clarity. She begins to doubt her path and ends up doubting her very self. As she spirals down through the abyss of uncertainty, she will undertake almost any action, however radical, to restore a sense of inner calm. In the United States, one of every three women is taking antidepressants. But the other two out of three often deal with their loss of innocence through consumption, the most addictive drug of all. What's left is a house filled with junk. Men don't cheat on their wives for sex but for an ego boost. Because they don't like who they are, they need a stranger to tell them that they matter. A woman who is not his wife praises his talents and he finds it impossible to resist her charms. And why not his wife? Because the man who thinks he is a loser sees the woman dumb enough to marry him as a loser squared. When we lose our innocence, even the most basic decisions become major trials and we feel confounded at every turn, resulting in more unhappiness and depression. It's a vicious cycle.

The ultimate cause of depression—when it is not chemical imbalance—is a feeling of meaninglessness. The secret to happiness is purposefulness.

At the same time, we are never more powerful than when we experience personal cohesion. Contentment and cheerfulness depend on an integrated personality. Humans need to feel whole. We need to know that there is only one master of our mental household. Nothing compartmentalizes us more than sin, and nothing synthesizes our personalities into one indivisible unit more than innocence.

Maimonides says he was once asked why Adam and Eve were seemingly rewarded for their sin. Only after their transgression of eating from the tree of knowledge of good and evil does it say "they came to know their nakedness." Before they sinned, they had no idea. They were oblivious. But sin brought them knowledge. And greater insight is a plus, right? An adaptation of Maimonides's response to that question is this: The reason Adam and Eve pranced around naked in the garden is that they had nothing to hide. They were totally innocent. They had no warts, no blemishes, no iniquity to conceal. They had no tarnishing stains to paper over with awards and degrees and designer labels. They felt beautiful just the way they were. That's what's meant when the Bible says they were naked and were not ashamed. They were not ashamed to be themselves. They didn't feel they needed titles before their names and initials after to be important. They didn't need fancy houses and Tiffany jewelry to feel loved. They required no external embellishments to prop themselves up.

But the moment they sinned, they felt ugly and naked. Like so many people today, they felt unworthy on their own merits. They needed to name-drop, hang out with the right crowd, join the jet-set elite. What a horrible feeling it is to feel as though you're not enough. Adam and Eve's newfound vulnerability resulted directly from feeling inadequate. This is hardly a reward. Ever since, humans have scrambled to hide their sense of deficiency.

When we are uncomfortable with who or what we are, or what we have become, we pretend to be something different. If Sarah and Rachel are friends, but Sarah gossips behind Rachel's back, the next time they meet, Sarah will be uncomfortable around Rachel. She can't be natural because she has something to hide. The real her, the element of her personality that dislikes Rachel and is a treacherous friend, must now remain concealed in public. By developing this split persona, Sarah gradually becomes unhinged from herself. And all because she has betrayed a friendship and now has something to conceal.

Once you have something serious to hide, you cannot be yourself, and of all the reasons for a husband and wife not to have an affair, that is the most important of all. The whole point of marriage is to have one person around whom you can always be comfortable. But your infidelity has made that impossible and now there is a deceptive unease even in this, the most intimate of relationships.

This compartmentalization is a great waste. The best way to succeed in life and to create human friendships is to allow our fullest personality to be manifest. Confidence is essential to both personal and professional success, and confidence cannot be grafted onto a self that is hiding something. Like the sun at high noon, the human personality is potentially warm, vibrant, and compelling enough to make every acquaintance into a friend. But when partially concealed, it loses its potency. We simply are not very effective in creating loving relationships with half our personality tied behind our backs.

Without innocence, there can be no peace. Without peace, there can likewise be no happiness.

In ancient Israel the day of Yom Kippur was witness to a ritual practiced every year in the temple in Jerusalem. The high priest would enter the Holy of Holies and carry out a special program of sacrificial offerings designed to bring about atonement on behalf of all Israel. If he were to make a single error in so holy a place, he could incur instant death. So when he emerged whole, a throng of thousands would accompany him, singing and dancing, to his home, where he would offer a celebratory feast. According to the prayer liturgy, when the high priest emerged from the Holy of Holies, he looked "like a bridegroom on the day of his wedding." In a word, he glowed.

The bridegroom glows on the day of his wedding because he is a new man embarking on a new life. Any mistakes he may have made prior to his life with his bride are in the past. His bride embraces him fully and he feels wonderful and whole. They are a new unit and he is a new man. He is as pure as on the day he was born.

When our sins are forgiven, we shine. Any impediment that separated our inner self from our outer self has been removed, and the light of our infinite soul can radiate unhindered. The innocent person shines even as she walks down the street, because her soul illuminates the entire person. The body is translucent, not cloudy, clear rather than frosty. The guilty person has allowed his body to become opaque. Rather than his personality serving as a window to the soul, it is now an obstacle, a brick wall that traps the soul's rays. Few people will ever discover the real person, and this is much to the guilty person's detriment. Only the radiation of the soul's inner fire can engender the warmth necessary for lasting friendships. A cold personality makes a chilling impact.

Yom Kippur is therefore a day to indulge the soul rather than the body. On Yom Kippur we neglect the needs of the body. All sensual pleasures, such as eating, lovemaking, and bathing, are prohibited and replaced by fasting, prayer, and basking in G-d's warmth. The body sloughs away. The soul is revealed in all its brilliance.

But if G-d is already so loving and compassionate, so prepared to forgive our iniquity, why the need for Yom Kippur? The ancient rabbis stated that although we must sincerely repent on the Day of Atonement, it is not our repentance that actually brings about forgiveness *but the day of Yom Kippur itself.* This view is taken much further by Rabbi Judah the

Prince, editor of the Mishnah and a highly influential figure, who maintained, even more astonishingly, that the power of the day of Yom Kippur is such that even if people do not repent, they are still forgiven for their sins!

How? Imagine a man who has built up an electronics store from scratch. He hires two new employees to help with sales: a stranger who applied off the street and his own son, whom he has taken on board to teach him the business. Both turn out to be disasters. They are lazy and late. He warns each to shape up, and when they don't, he fires them. Months go by after he has replaced them with more competent staff. Father's Day arrives, and his son sends him a card, telling him how much he loves him. The very next day the father rehires his son. Meanwhile, the other fired employee writes a letter apologizing for his negligence. But he is not rehired. What's the critical difference? They are being judged by two different standards. A son receives preferential treatment, whereas a stranger does not. When the father related to his son as an employee, his son was found negligent and given the boot. He had spoiled the relationship with his boss through shoddy work and unaccountability.

But the moment Father's Day came around and the son, through the simple gesture of sending a card, reminded the father that he was not a stranger, but his own flesh and blood, the father no longer construed his son's tardiness as a major infraction. After all, the whole reason the father works is for his family. How can he fire his own son? Sometimes he needs a little reminder that his son is everything he lives for. So the moment the son reminded his father that he is not just any employee, his negligence is forgiven, treated as if it had never happened. In the face of the infinite bond that connects father and son, the boy's mistakes are utterly immaterial.

The same is true of our relationship with G-d. In the Bible G-d is referred to both as king and father. And humanity is referred to both as servants as well as children. "You are children to the Lord your G-d." Throughout the year G-d relates to us as master to a servant, as a boss to his worker. "We humans are all workers committed to spreading light," the Talmud declares. Humans are born to fulfill a mission: to pursue love, promote justice, and serve G-d faithfully. We have a task to complete, and when we transgress the central tenets of our covenant with G-d, or when we fail to live up to our calling, we become like negligent employees facing dismissal.

But on Yom Kippur, the whole world achieves elevation. G-d is closer to humanity and humanity is closer to G-d. The special parent-child relationship between the Almighty and humanity is manifest. At this exalted plane, what would have constituted a sin for a servant is simply nonexistent. The moment we show G-d our unbridled love for Him— through our passionate devotion in prayer and fasting—He embraces us, as a loving parent, and the transgressions that divided us are utterly inconsequential. If a Jew makes just a minimal effort, a minimal commitment of coming to synagogue and fasting and showing G-d that he cares, although he may ignore many of the precepts throughout the year, G-d sees that this is His child, and through this act of commitment all the bad is automatically forgotten.

Is there an exception to this rule of repentance? More than two hundred years ago, a young Hassidic man traveled all the way across Russia to see the great Rabbi Levi Yitzchak of Berditchev, a sage noted for his great love of all G-d's creatures. In an age in which many rabbis were known for fire-and-brimstone oratory, Rabbi Yitzchak felt love for the righteous man and sinner alike. The young man was ushered into the rabbi's study. "Rebbe," he said, "I have sinned, and I have come to you for guidance about how to seek atonement. You see, there was a married woman after whom I lusted and she after me. To my eternal shame, we consummated our mutual attraction. I have come to you in guilt to expiate my sin. But before you tell me what penitence I may undertake, know that the sin was not so bad as it could have been. You see, before we acted on our desire, she went to the *mikveh* [the ritual bath in which a woman immerses herself after menstruation]. So at least she was ritually clean."

Upon hearing the man's confession, the rabbi rose from behind his desk and commanded the young man to leave his office immediately. "It is best that you go, for I cannot help you." The young man was confused. "I came to see you specifically," he pleaded. "I could have been shunned by so many other rabbis. But you have a reputation for tolerance and loving kindness. Did I make a mistake traveling for days to see you?"

"I am tolerant and loving," replied the rabbi, "to most people. Because people on the whole are good. It's just that they sin and do foolish things that derail their lives, and I am here to help them on the difficult journey back to innocence. But you are different. You are not someone who sinned. You, my son, are a sinner. Had you told me that you found yourself in a room with a beautiful woman and you could not control yourself, I would have told you, *Nu, Gei veiter*, 'Get on with your life.' Move forward. Put the sin behind you. Forget about it, and wash it away in a sea of good deeds. But this is not what happened. Rather, you said that she first went to the mikveh. In other words, this was not an act of passion. It was an act of premeditated sin. You planned your transgression. Both of you began your countdown after her period commenced. Five days till we sin, four days, three days, and so forth. So I cannot instruct you as to how to purge yourself of what you have done. Your attempt to whitewash your sin has relegated you to the ranks of the incorrigible. You and your sin are one."

We make mistakes. We can rest in the confidence that we will be forgiven. But we must always be on the alert never to rationalize our mistakes, removing the natural barrier that should separate our mistakes from our person. To err is human, but to make peace with our errors is unforgivable.

CHAPTER 18

Weaning Ourselves Off Violence

∞∞∞∞∞∞∞∞∞∞∞

*The Lord is good to all and His tender mercies are
over all His creatures.*

—PSALMS 145:9

*The greatness of a nation and its moral progress
can be judged by the way its animals are treated.*

—MAHATMA GANDHI

According to the kabbalah, every human being is possessed of two natures. We have a G-dly nature and an animal nature, an innate spiritual impulse and a materialistic impulse. Our animal nature is not a bad
thing, and indeed without our lusts, passions, and instincts, no man would
ever marry a woman or build a home. No woman would love passionate
sex or allow her husband to draw near her. We would not care about our
appearance and would care even less about our material well-being.

Our animal nature is potent and powerful. King Solomon says cryp-
tically in the book of Proverbs: "There is much wheat in the strength of
an ox." But it has dangers. That is obvious. If we don't channel our sexual

appetites into marriage, we invite disaster. If we don't channel our love of money into charity and philanthropy, we will grow selfish and boring. That's what Jewish values teach us to do—not to repress our animal natures, for without them we would lose our productivity, but to channel them into moral directions.

We need values that push our robustness away from aggression and toward benevolence. This is actually a rather controversial position today. Some social anthropologists suggest that the vast amount of violence in television and films is actually of therapeutic value. So too organized sports, the argument goes. The cheering crowd can spur on its team to destroy a foe on the playing field rather than hacking one another to death with machetes. This outlet allows society to rid itself of its primal instinct for violence.

I find this reasoning highly suspect. Humans need a code of conduct to purge them from the instinct for violence and to condition them to receive as great a thrill from altruistic action as from inflicting injury. Long ago, Judaism devised a program to wean man from his appetite for violence. It has many parts but is found primarily in the Jewish laws of kosher food.

First, the facts: Jewish dietary laws mandate that a Jew may eat only those animals that chew their cud and have split hooves. The only marine animals that may be consumed are those with fins and scales. Among birds, the Torah prohibits twenty-four types, but the common denominator is that birds of prey are not kosher. The Torah forbids consuming predatory animals and those that did not care for their young. The mixing of meat and milk is forbidden. Most important, the laws prohibit eating blood and mandate that any animal is kosher only if it has been slaughtered at the neck.

These laws seem so strangely precise, even archaic, that many have tried to come up with an explanation that makes more sense to the modern brain. Kosher food was legislated for hygienic reasons, they'll say. Some believe that the ban on eating pork is because it can lead to trichinosis, and that shellfish was forbidden because of the dangerous bacteria they contain. And although there are definite health benefits to eating kosher food, which is why statistics show that 20 percent of Americans look for kosher symbols at the supermarket, these are all secondary concerns.

These laws were designed by G-d to communicate values. With their extreme emphasis on the humane slaughter of animals, they condition us to detest death, abhor blood, and recoil from unnecessarily hurting any of G-d's creatures. Love for sadistic pleasures must be utterly uprooted from the human heart. G-d is the Creator of life, and man is its guardian and protector. A man who delights in blood sport distances himself from G-d.

In the Bible, preventing unnecessary pain to animals is a cornerstone of divine ethics. Humans were given dominion over the animals only to increase the quality of human life and to serve the Creator. So, sure, you can attach a plow to an ox or a saddle to a horse to lessen your workload. But what can one say about a society in which animals are mistreated as a form of human amusement? Such abuse is called *tzaar baalei hayyim*, "distress to living creatures." The ancient rabbis decreed that one must feed one's cattle before feeding oneself, and even the Ten Commandments include domestic animals in the Sabbath rest. One of the original seven laws given to Noah's children, and thus to all mankind, was a severe prohibition against sadistic treatment of animals.

Jewish values also utterly reject hunting. Taking animal life as a recreational pastime is abhorrent, a sin against G-d. The only justification for hunting is to obtain food for human survival. My Jewish-values upbringing made me feel uncomfortable when I first lived in Great Britain and observed highly cultured, civilized men and women taking obvious delight in shooting innocent animals, or when I saw foxes being torn to bits by dogs on a foxhunt.

Okay, so here's the obvious question: If the kosher laws are designed to instill an appreciation for animal life and a detestation of violence and the sight of blood, why not be vegan? That's a good question. The truth is that vegetarianism is what the Bible originally mandated. Adam and Eve were in fact commanded never to take the life of any animal but to subsist on fruit and vegetables alone. "From all the trees of the Garden you may eat." There was no mention of animals. But after the flood, things changed. The flood killed all plant life. The only things left were the animals Noah had brought into the ark. Had G-d not permitted Noah and his family to eat animals, they would have perished. Moreover, since Noah had worked so hard to save the animals, he was entitled to use them to survive. He had saved them and they in turn saved him. Ever since, meat has been allowed as a source of nutrients.

But once you allow people to kill animals, you run the risk of desensitizing them to death and violence. Have you ever been to a slaughterhouse? It can be pretty gruesome. On my trip to Zimbabwe with a Christian relief organization, we purchased ten goats so we could make a destitute village a Thanksgiving feast. They slaughtered them in front of my eyes, severing the animals' heads and then butchering the animals into small pieces. Everything was then placed in a giant pot. I was having a hard time watching all this—but not the villagers, for whom this was a common practice (that is, on the rare occasions when they were able to afford meat). So how do we ensure that amid killing animals we do not become inured to the practices of violence? In other words, how does one partake of the animal's flesh without becoming one himself?

G-d gave man kashruth to establish clear rules about which animals could be used for food and how they could be put to death, and which parts of the animal could be eaten. You don't kill a cucumber when you eat it. But you kill an animal. And there must be strict regulations with regards to taking an animal's life. You can't eat its blood. You have to pour it into the ground, a point I really appreciated while in Zimbabwe. The villagers drained all the goat's blood and put it into a bowl for the dogs. To be honest, the sight tied my stomach in knots. But we're *supposed* to feel a bit queasy when we see blood—not to enjoy it.

Seen in this light, the kosher laws are the perfect compromise between being a vegetarian and being an omnivore. Of course, being a vegetarian is far better and if you make that choice, more power to you. Taking an animal's life is a concession at best, and one that needs to be regulated.

There's more. That the laws of kosher food rule out all beasts of prey teaches another values-based lesson. Animals that have split hooves cannot be predators because this characteristic makes them slow-moving and awkward, unable to run and pursue other animals as the swifter hunters with paws can. All animals that chew their cud, and are thus permitted, are herbivores that spend a great deal of their time standing and chewing. They often have minimal teeth, but a rough palate, which allows them to eat grass and other foliage. When they swallow a vegetable, they cannot digest it, not having chewed it sufficiently, so the food travels to the first of their four stomachs, where the somatic acids break it down further. After the food has passed through two stomachs, it is driven up the gullet again, chewed for a second time, and then led through the other two stomachs. As the ancient rabbis point out, the permitted animals spend a great deal of time digesting their food and display almost plantlike passivity. They readily submit to human domination.

What the Torah was doing in limiting Jews to passive, vegetarian animals was, first, weaning them from a love of violence by causing them to slaughter animals humanely and, second, ensuring that they did not consume anything that would encourage their innate predatory streak. Omnivorous and carnivorous, flesh-eating animals are thus not allowed.

In the New Testament, Jesus is quoted as saying, "It is not what goes into the mouth that defiles a person. It is what comes out of the mouth that defiles." There is some truth to this. Purity of language, refraining from gossip—these are all very important Jewish values. Speech is a uniquely human trait that should not be defiled. But Jewish values maintain that what goes into the mouth *is* nonetheless important. People can compromise their holiness by absorbing foods that bring out aggression. In contemporary times we've learned all too well that eating unhealthy foods leads to health risks. Well, the soul has its healthy and unhealthy foods as well. If you eat poison, it can kill you. And from a Jewish values perspective, certain foods are poisonous to the soul.

In my book on dreams, I wrote of the effects of strong somatic stimuli on our mental processes. Studies show that people who eat spicy foods often have violent dreams and nightmares, caused by toxins and the vapors of strong, acidic fare. The same has been proven true about thinking. The vapors arising from strong foods may impede or stimulate thought. Similarly, it has long been established that certain foods can act as aphrodisiacs. Foods can and do affect our thought processes.

The kosher laws forbid shellfish for precisely this reason. "Now the reason for specifying fins and scales is that fish which have fins and scales get nearer to the surface of the water and are found more generally in freshwater areas," the great medieval scholar Nahmanides explained. "Those without fins and scales usually live in the lower muddy strata which are exceedingly moist and where there is no heat. They breed in musty swamps and eating them can be injurious to health." Shellfish live on the bottom of the sea, where they act as scavengers, consuming all the waste, debris, and refuse. They are therefore viewed as both physically and spiritually injurious. The Bible commands us to be healthy and to guard "your soul exceedingly well."

That we are what we eat already resonates with the American people. I mentioned above that although Jews represent only 2 percent of America's population, 20 percent of the people living in this country look for kosher symbols when buying food. They know that kosher food is a symbol of healthy living, both physically and spiritually.

We also cannot eat any animal that has not been humanely slaughtered at the neck. Judaism's special method of slaughtering animals, called *shehitah,* consists of an incision made across the neck of the animal or fowl by a person trained for ritual slaughter. A special razor-sharp knife with a smooth edge, with absolutely no nicks, is used to prevent tearing of the animal's gullet. The cut must be made by moving the knife in a single swift and uninterrupted sweep, not by pressure or by stabbing. The cut severs the main arteries, rendering the animal unconscious and permitting the blood to drain from the body. The ritual slaughterer (*shohet*) recites a prayer before the act of shehitah.

Going back to my African experience, the villagers used a knife that was not that sharp, requiring many passes to kill the animal. It was gruesome to watch. Later, one of the villagers told me that a few weeks earlier they had even used a butter knife to slaughter a goat when they could not find something sharper. This would be severely prohibited by Jewish values. If the animal suffers in the slightest, the meat is not kosher.

Shehitah results in immediate loss of consciousness, and any movement afterward is only muscle reflex. In short, the animal does not suffer. Similarly, the Bible declares that right after the slaughter, one must pour out all the blood into the earth and to salt the animal until all the blood is removed from the meat. Red meat filled with blood—even that of a kosher animal ritually killed—is forbidden since the Almighty insists that we abhor blood in every form.

From a values perspective, once you become desensitized to the value of animal life, you are but a short step away from having contempt for human life. We often hear that murderers and rapists used to shoot BB guns at cats.

The opposite is also true. From a values perspective, we dare not elevate animal life to parity with human life. People were justifiably outraged that Leona Helmsley left $12 million in her estate to her dog. There are too many hungry children in the world for that. Likewise, many people in America give their pets all of their time, to the detriment of human relationships. Yes, I know dogs are man's best friend. But let's be serious. A pet's companionship will never equal that of a human and we should not confuse the two. Americans love their pets. My family loves our pets just as much. But we have to love people even more.

So the Jewish values perspective is that animals have absolute rights. They cannot be hunted for sport, abused, or mistreated. But they do not rise to the level of people and should not supplant human company.

As I've said, the kosher laws are primarily about inculcating values. The Torah highlights the image of G-d in man, a feat that can be accomplished only if man's animal nature does not overwhelm his higher self. Kosher food serves as a strong bulwark in the fight against our carnality and overindulgence in material pursuits. It reminds us that our obligation is always to life.

CHAPTER 19

Choose Life

ᴏᴏᴏᴏᴏᴏᴏᴏᴏᴏᴏᴏᴏᴏ

There are a thousand thousand reasons to live this life, every one of them sufficient.
　　　—MARILYNNE ROBINSON, *Gilead*

One day your life will flash before your eyes. Make sure it's worth watching.
　　　　　—ANONYMOUS

I left one element of kosher laws unexplained. We Jews do not eat cheeseburgers or other mixtures of dairy and meat products. Mixing, eating, or cooking milk and meat together is prohibited. There is a profound reason behind this seemingly obtuse rule: Milk is a symbol of life, the very elixir sustaining our early and innocent existence. Dead meat, however, is death incarnate. They are irreconcilable opposites. And Jewish values, more than anything else, are a celebration of life.

Many ancient civilizations promoted the culture of death. In Egypt pharaohs spent their lives preparing giant mausoleums that would celebrate them in death. We know many of them today as the giant pyramids.

Similarly, human sacrifice, even child sacrifice, was common throughout the ancient world. Go to Chichen Itza on the Yucatan peninsula in Mexico and you will see giant Mayan pyramids that were used to slaughter thousands in rituals of human sacrifice. That's why the Jewish values formulated at the time were so strongly designed to wean people from death: The Jews were trying to build a culture of life.

And we need a reinforcement of life. Let's face it. With so much depression today, with so many broken lives, many people do not believe that life is an intrinsic blessing. I have counseled many people who think life is a curse that some wish to terminate. Jewish values reject morbidity utterly. Our values are always positive. No nation has suffered as much as the Jews. But because of our values, we have always remained passionate about life. Others raise a glass and say, "Cheers," or "Salud," but the Jews have always said, "L'Chaim!" *To life!*

Death may be inevitable, but it has to be resisted with every ounce of energy. Life, even in its most painful manifestations, presents endless opportunity. But death brings only monotony, an inability to change or progress. In death we lose all our uniqueness. We move from the animate to the inanimate, from flesh to stone.

Life, from the perspective of Jewish values, is everything that is G-dly, everything that is noble. In the Bible G-d is referred to as the G-d of life. The Torah is described as the tree of life. As a river is connected to the spring whence it stems, the living individual is connected with the eternal source of life. Death comes about when the connection has been severed. Death, rather than a state of being, is a void, a black hole, a vacuum of meaning and existence. Death is the darkness that ensues once the light has gone out. There are no wakes in Judaism. The dead are buried quickly, with a quiet and solemn dignity, and we await the time when all will be raised from the dust.

Death, from a Jewish values perspective, is not its own state. Rather, it is the absence of life. And we dare not accord a cavernous emptiness a value that it does not deserve. We have to convince people as to the blessing of life. We need them to embrace life at all times.

Moses says in the Bible, "This day I call heaven and earth as witnesses against you that I have set before you life and death, blessings and curses. Now choose life, so that you and your children may live" (Deuteronomy 30:19). We are enjoined at all times to choose life. We dare never despair.

One episode of my TV show, *Shalom in the Home,* featured Carolyn, a woman in her thirties whose husband was killed in a terrible car crash as they were driving back from Valentine's Day dinner. There was a morbid air in the home. The pictures of her husband hanging on the wall were dark and ominous. She refused to date, so consumed was she by grief. She and her two young daughters sat and watched endless reels of her husband on video. My job was to try to bring her back to the land of the living.

I sat her down. "Carolyn, the Bible said 3,000 years ago that you have to choose life. Unfortunately, sometimes death chooses us. We're driving in a car with someone we love and death storms down the street. The car veers out of control and death strikes. It claims a victim. Death overpowers us and forces its way into our lives. There is nothing we can do to stop it. It becomes an unwelcome visitor. It stays in our home and it lingers. But our job is to push him out. We don't want death in our homes, we don't want death in our lives. Even as it imposes itself, our role is to make death feel unwelcome. We do that by choosing life.

"In your case death barged through your door. You didn't choose it. It chose you. But you made the mistake of inviting him in and making him feel welcome. You made him feel at home. Now he lives comfortably among you and your daughters. You are choosing death rather than choosing life. It's time to stop. He has claimed enough victims in this family. You cannot allow him to claim you even as the blood courses through your veins. You cannot allow yourself to become the living dead. Shoo him out. Show him the door. Choose life and abandon death."

Carolyn, I'm happy to say, reoriented her thoughts and home. We exchanged the black-and-white morbid pictures of the children's dad for color photos of him smiling while holding his babies. Carolyn began to devote her life to a women's education group that she still runs today. She is a remarkable woman, charming, insightful, and an incredible mother, and she remains one of my family's closest friends.

Life represents attachment to the living G-d, while death represents a divine absence. We have to wean ourselves from a belief that life and death can coexist. Humans must remain firmly dedicated toward combating darkness wherever it may appear. Our homes and material possessions proclaim the line that divides the living from the dead, the eternal from the ephemeral, the blessed from the cursed.

Judaism always seeks to separate life from death. Although we humans are at times overtaken by death, we must still run from it with all our soul, with all our might. Jewish ritual is designed to reinforce the light and contain the darkness. Observing Jewish values establishes a perimeter into which death cannot infiltrate. A kohen (member of the priestly class), who administers to the living G-d, is forbidden to come into contact with a dead body or attend a funeral, except that of a close relative. Since his being is dedicated to the sacred service in the Holy Temple, bestowing life and blessing on the congregation of Israel, it is inappropriate that he should be exposed to the antithesis of life.

Churches traditionally were ringed with cemeteries. Similarly, the treasures of the great European cathedrals consist of relics of the saints—their fingers, hands, and vials of blood. One great medieval cathedral I visited even contains the head of St. Catherine of Siena, displayed for all visitors to see. I have seen churches in Europe and South America containing catacombs filled with tens of thousands of bones. This could never happen in a synagogue. No cemetery is allowed anywhere near the synagogue and in fact Jewish cemeteries have to be outside the city walls.

Contrary to popular belief, Judaism repudiates martyrdom. Jews have not chosen to be martyrs throughout the ages but rather it has been forced upon them. The Bible is clear: "Choose life," not death. Jewish values enjoin us to make the world more loving and just. This is a task for the living, not for the dead. Because of its "this-world orientation," Judaism would never contend that G-d is more easily found in the heavens than on earth. Seeking death, therefore, to bask under the heavenly throne is a misguided effort. Jews are probably the most martyred people of all time, but even so there are only three commandments in the Torah where a Jewish person is obligated to lay down his life: idolatry, sexual immorality, and murder. If someone forces you to commit any of these, you have to be ready to forfeit your life. But otherwise, you are obligated to choose life.

To be sure, those who have been martyred for their faith are accorded a special place in the religion. They are the holy ones who paid the ultimate price for their spiritual allegiance, but this is a de facto acceptance after the martyrdom. Judaism has no tradition of saints who exalted their position by intentionally choosing death when life was still an option. With rare exceptions, all the giants of Jewish history attained their lofty status through their example and teachings while alive. Martyrdom is something to be endured if necessary, never something to be sought out.

In its attitude toward martyrdom, Judaism is radically different from religions such as early Christianity and especially Islam, which encourage their followers to seek martyrdom. From Jesus onward to many of the great saints, martyrdom is glorified in Christianity, and its very symbol is the cross of the Son of G-d martyred for his beliefs.

Judaism, and the values it promotes, is profoundly a religion of life. "L'Chaim" says it well: "To life." Not even good life, or happy life, just life—because life itself is an unconditional blessing. Judaism celebrates life to the fullest, and its greatest promise, by the ancient prophets, is that one day all death shall be defeated: "And he will destroy on this mountain the shroud that is cast over all peoples, the sheet that is spread over all nations; he will swallow up death forever."

CHAPTER 20

Respect for Women

In the degradation of women, the very fountains of life are poisoned at their source.

—LUCRETIA MOTT

There will never be a new world order until women are a part of it.

—ALICE PAUL

Until the giving of the Torah, people loved only their own relatives or their countrymen and kinfolk—those to whom they had blood ties or with whom they shared a common identity. Common interests trumped common values. In one stroke, the Torah commanded people to love the stranger, the orphan, and the widow and to protect the interests of the vulnerable. Might did *not* make right. G-d's providence spread like a canopy over all of creation, protecting the weak and oppressed. The Almighty legislated punishment for those who took advantage of the unfortunate and those who lacked natural protectors.

The Torah forbade employers to exploit their employees and insisted that wages never be withheld. It mandated a comprehensive social welfare system in which every man and woman of commerce was obligated to deliver at least 10 percent of profits to the poor. It made marrying a woman against her will illegal and imposed extremely harsh penalties on rape. Jewish values also restructured the social order, establishing a priestly class to replace the warrior class as the nation's leaders. The pursuit of love and justice was enshrined as humankind's highest goal. The Jews proclaimed that all humans were created in G-d's image and were bound by a divine, loving moral code.

The injection of Jewish values into the world order was the greatest revolution of all time. But what is not always appreciated is that it was a *feminine* revolution. Indeed, all of Judaism can be seen as the long-term introduction of feminine values in place of masculine ones. Men won't ever be fully sensitive to the full reality of G-d unless they harness their inner feminine energy. Only reducing his aggression and competitiveness can redeem a man from his self-centeredness and focus him fully on G-d.

We discussed this in Chapter 5. But some questions about the full implications of the superiority of the feminine were left unanswered, questions that plagued me throughout the eleven years I served as rabbi at Oxford University. Many students saw Jewish values as discriminatory against women. Some female students avoided Orthodox services because they didn't want to be segregated from the men during prayers. They cited many other Jewish policies concerning women, including the traditional prohibition against women becoming rabbis or leading worship in the synagogue.

In all these things, the students were right. The obligations placed on men and women under Jewish law *are* distinct. And in an age in which success outside the home is most prized, Jewish values, with its traditionally more private and nurturing role for women, appears chauvinistic. Men are obligated to keep all the commandments of the Torah, whereas women are absolved from any commandment that is time-dependent, such as wearing a prayer shawl, reciting the three daily prayers, and lighting the Chanukah menorah. Commandments incumbent on both men and women, such as eating kosher food and giving to charity, apply at all times of the day and year. But women are relieved from reciting the evening prayer, the *maariv*.

"Why are we hidden behind the *mechitza*, the synagogue divider?" some young students asked me as they noisily left our prayer services, never to return. "Why can't I get up in front of the congregation and have an *aliyah*?" they asked, referring to the call to the Torah, reserved exclusively for men in Orthodox synagogues. "Why must women dress modestly and remain locked behind layers of clothing?" This spilled over into more comprehensive complaints. Why the general Jewish attitude of separating the sexes? Why do Jewish values insist on so many safeguards in friendships between the sexes, such as prohibiting men and women from being together in a locked private room unless they are married? In short, how can Jewish values insist that the feminine is superior and still insist on separating women from men?

To unwrap these questions, I would start with even more basic ones: Why do women exist at all? Why men? The Creator could have made the world with only one gender reproducing asexually. But the ancient Jewish mystics explained that the differences between men and women are far from meaningless and arbitrary. According to the kabbalah, the sexes are not equal. Rather, women stem from a loftier spiritual source than men. They mature sooner, they have more naturally refined characters, more spiritual dispositions, a greater inclination toward fidelity and commitment in relationships, and a general reluctance to engage in physical violence. The ancient rabbis adopted the idea of a greater capacity for focus in women, as well as a more fully developed spiritual intuition.

The Talmud declares that a woman is a man's greatest blessing and that a man without a wife lives without joy, blessing, and good. A man should love his wife as himself and respect her more than himself. When Rabbi Joseph heard his mother's footsteps, he would say, "Let me arise before the approach of the Shekhinah (the divine presence)." The rabbis said that Israel was redeemed from Egypt by virtue of its righteous women. They further declared that a man must be careful never to slight his wife when speaking to her, because women are sensitive to wrong, and that women have greater faith and deeper spirituality than men.

As the kabbalah explains, women, represented by a circle (the female anatomy), flow out from their higher source in the transcendent G-d of creation. Women are above time. On the other hand, men stem from G-d's finite and limited light, women from His infinite light. Represented by a line (the male anatomy), men are time-bound and find their spiritual source in the G-d of history. That is why, the rabbis argued, men must wear the *talit katan* (mini prayer shawl) to remind them at all times of G-d's commandments, as well as the tefillin, which places G-d's words upon the mind and heart. Women do not need external reminders. G-d's words are actually written on their hearts and embedded in their souls. Women are far more conscious of G-d as an internal experience, where He is one with their being.

Here we begin to see the reasons for the separation. The female body and the female nature point to a "feminine mystique." Women are ultimately unknowable to a man, guaranteeing the male's eternal pursuit of the feminine. In other words, what draws a man to a woman is not that she is the same as him, but rather that she is his opposite. Erotic attraction depends on the need to overcome the obstacle of gender, a process we call obstacle seduction. Since married life and the family are the hallmarks of Jewish communal living, the Bible took extraordinary steps to ensure the continued attraction between the sexes and thereby the viability of long-term male-female relationships. Maintaining these differences is essential in sustaining this gravitation of opposites. Judaism always kept women in a slightly more screened-off state so they would not suffer overexposure and compromise an eternal touch of inscrutability. A woman who dresses modestly elicits great passion from a man simply by undressing. Very few women need their husbands to dress up in lingerie for them, but men often require these visual inducements to heighten attraction.

The masculine way focuses on improving all the world's imperfections. So the Torah gives men mitzvot involving a physical object a man can elevate to a higher state of perfection. But the feminine way of looking at the world entails seeing not the demons, but the angels, not the world's darkness, but its light. So the Jewish religion has given women mitzvot designed to bring forth more light. A woman's perhaps best-known mitzvah is lighting Sabbath candles every Friday evening. She is symbolically stating that the house is beautiful already; what it needs is to be illuminated so its beauty can be seen. A wife teaches her husband to remove the dark glasses of cynicism, giving him radiance and hope. A woman finds goodness in her man even when others see only his shortcomings.

One of the central ideas of the kabbalah is that the woman embodies the Shekhinah, the divine presence, commanding increased respect. The Zohar, the key work of Jewish mysticism, says in a famous passage:

> It is incumbent on a man to be ever "male and female" [married] in order that his faith may be firm, and that the Shekhinah may never depart from him. What, then, you will say, of a man who goes on a journey and, being absent from his wife, is no longer "male and female"? His remedy is to pray to G-d before he starts his journey, while he is still "male and female," in order to draw to himself the presence of his Maker. . . . When he does return home again, it is his duty to give his wife pleasure, because it was she who acquired for him his heavenly partner.

In this beautiful passage the Zohar affirms the need for husbands to be completed by their wives.

In the same vein, Rabbi Isaac Luria used to kiss his mother's hands on the eve of the Sabbath, the feminine component of the week. In his

circle the custom arose of reciting a chapter from Proverbs on Friday
night in praise of the Shekhinah. Jewish men sing it to their wives every
Sabbath eve. Eventually the custom was adopted by Jewish men far removed from kabbalism, who recited the passage in honor of their wives,
forgetting the custom's origin. To this day, one of the most moving events
of the Sabbath ritual is when a husband looks at his wife and recites to
her the tribute to a wife of excellence, the Aishet Chayil passage, attributed by tradition to King Solomon:

> A capable wife who can find? She is far more precious than jewels.
> The heart of her husband trusts in her, and he will have no lack of
> gain. She opens her hand to the poor, and reaches out her hands to
> the needy. Strength and dignity are her clothing, and she laughs at
> the time to come. She opens her mouth with wisdom, and the
> teaching of kindness is on her tongue. Her children rise up and call
> her happy; her husband too, and he praises her: "Many women have
> done excellently, but you surpass them all." Charm is deceitful, and
> beauty is vain, but a woman who fears the Lord is to be praised.

We must not misconstrue woman's more private role within Judaism
as secondary. Since a man does not immediately see G-d's light in the
world, he must immerse himself in an environment where even *he* experiences the presence of G-d. This is why only men are required to attend
religious services. Divine ritual becomes an alarm clock, ringing and alerting men to wake up and smell the coffee. Women, however, are more capable of discovering the hidden within the apparent. Those who have
spiritual fulfillment do not need to shout it from the pulpits of the synagogues any more than those who are truly in love need to indulge in communal displays of affection. Subtle dignity and quiet spirituality are far
more formidable. True religious piety and holiness do not holler. They
speak in a strong and steady voice, resonating from within.

Just imagine what our world would be like if the Jewish value of the feminine being superior to the masculine were universally embraced? Imagine if many in the Islamic world abandoned the masculine-aggressive religious posture and embraced a more nurturing religious role? Almost instantly Islam would be restored to its scholarly and humanitarian past. Imagine if such tyrants as Kim Jong Il and Mahmoud Ahmadinejad would be utterly repudiated by a world that no longer believed in strongmen. Imagine if we finally rejected militarism as a form of honor. So many more around the world would be free. I visited Zimbabwe in November 2009 and was spooked by the fear engendered in the population by its brutal dictator, Robert Mugabe. But just imagine if the world had ganged up on him for impoverishing his people and slaughtering his political opponents because we had committed ourselves once and for all to a more feminine spirit.

Closer to home, imagine a world where masculine honor was defined as fidelity to one woman rather than rampant sexual conquests. Imagine a world where husbands who made a few dollars and immediately dumped the devoted wife of twenty-five years in favor of the hot young thing felt a measure of social censure. Imagine a world where young men were taught from the outset that the cornerstone of manliness is the respect a gentleman shows a woman. Our university campuses would be radically different places. They would not be characterized by rampant womanizing and the distribution of condoms. Young people would start dating one another rather than hooking up. Women would not feel the need to sexualize their bodies or drink themselves to oblivion in order to gain male attention.

To the contrary. The pressure would be on men to act like gentlemen to be worthy of women. The men rather than the women would do the heavy lifting in relationships. Three-quarters of all divorces today are initiated by women, and this is largely a function of how unhappy women are in relationships. Our marriages would be stronger because our wives would be happier. Children would be raised in more nurturing environments where they would not feel constant pressure to produce good grades at school to feel loved. Our kids would be healthier and more secure. We wouldn't hear stories of parents assaulting referees at Little League games, because the winning or losing would be subordinate to simply playing fair and enjoying the journey. If we were to extol the Jewish value of the feminine-passive over the masculine-aggressive we would live in a healthier, more peaceful and humble world.

One last question from my Oxford students needs to be addressed: Why the separation in prayer? In most world religions, institutionalized prayer is a moment of profound security. One sits with one's spouse and children in the place of worship and sings inspirational hymns that overwhelm the senses and satiate the spirit. Not so in Orthodox Judaism, where a visible divider separates men and women during prayer. As a pragmatic religion, Judaism understands that a visible man or woman may distract us from the invisible G-d. Prayer requires intense concentration. But in this age of liberalism and egalitarianism, separation of men and women in prayer still makes people uncomfortable.

Once I hosted a Jewish Nobel laureate and his wife at our home for the Sabbath. His wife was extremely friendly, but she made it clear that she would not attend our prayer services. "When we married, my husband was Orthodox and we prayed at a *shul* with a divider. I got tired of sitting alone behind the curtain," she told me. Ever since then they had prayed at a conservative synagogue where couples sat together. "I will not attend your synagogue and be a party to discrimination against women," she told me. "But what about people like my mother?" I responded. "After her divorce, my mother raised five children on her own. The one party to whom she could turn and pour out her troubled heart was G-d, every Sabbath at the synagogue. Should she be reminded of her unpartnered state every time she came to synagogue? Should she have to look around and see all the blissfully married women and be made to feel like a pariah? And what of the men and women who cannot remedy the problem of sitting alone, because they are widowed, divorced, or just plain single?" I asked. "Shall they be reminded of their loneliness every time they enter the synagogue?" To this she had scarcely a response.

I could increase the number of people who participate in our prayer services tenfold if I simply got rid of the *mechitza*, the partition separating men and women. But then I would not attract those people to whom prayer is most important and who have the greatest need to pray: the men and especially the women who have not yet been fortunate enough to find a full-time partner in life or to start a family. It is to their needs that a synagogue must cater. A house of worship is no place for someone who is single or bereaved to feel even lonelier.

Men and women, husbands and wives, sit separately during the prayer services because prayer is not about feeling security but about loneliness, dread, despair, and helplessness. Prayer is not a time for a person to feel that his family is his greatest blessing. Nor is prayer inspired when feeling surrounded by the consoling presence of intimate loved ones. "From the depths I called to you, Lord"—the psalmist reminds us that real prayer takes place when we cry out to G-d, not from the broad spaces, but from the abyss. Man prays to G-d upon experiencing his own sense of vulnerability.

A few years ago, a young woman wrote to tell me that it was tragic that the potent feminine energy was not being used to heal a broken planet. I couldn't agree more. It is the women of the world who will cure us of the insecurity of masculine aggression. Surely this should be a high goal of today's women, to help topple the walls separating spirit from matter and soul from body, to finally bring true harmony between masculine and feminine energies, and to teach men that they don't have to always prove themselves competitively to be worthy. Men think within dualistic structures that are always at odds, but women approach life more holistically and harmoniously. Men perceive a rupture in existence. They see evil and rush to vanquish it. Women take a higher view and perceive the possibility of union within all that is.

The feminine energy is one of repair and sharing. Women today, with their higher and more immediate powers of spiritual insight, can teach the world the relevance of religion to contemporary life and help mankind discover our spiritual potential. Women cannot accomplish this if they use men as their spiritual role models.

CHAPTER 21

Chosenness

It is too little, he says, for you to be my servant, to raise up the tribes of Jacob, and restore the survivors of Israel; I will make you a light to the nations, that my salvation may reach to the ends of the earth.

—ISAIAH 49:6

He who pursues fame will lose his name.

—HILLEL

The Bible teaches that the Jews were chosen by G-d—but for what? To disseminate the knowledge of G-d and His demands for righteous action, the Jews were given a mandate to spread morality and G-dly ethics. Not surprisingly, many people came to perceive the Jews as a danger to their lifestyles. The powerful, after all, often prefer to remain corrupt. The selfish prefer to remain selfish. And here were Jewish values, proposing a revolutionary redirection of human will.

Whatever virtue being the chosen nation has conferred upon the Jews, it has also served as an endless cause of grief. The idea of chosenness was the original cause of anti-Semitism. Individuals hell-bent on destroying the Jewish nation, such as Haj Amin el-Husseini, the mufti of Jerusalem who admired Hitler, used Jewish chosenness to foment hatred: "The overwhelming egoism which lies in the character of the Jews, their unworthy belief that they are G-d's chosen nation and their assertion that all was created for them and that other people are animals [makes them] incapable of being trusted. They cannot mix with any other nation but live as parasites among the nations, suck out their blood, embezzle their property, corrupt their morals." George Bernard Shaw proposed that the Nazi idea of Aryan racial superiority merely mimicked the Jewish value of chosenness.

Claims to being special are not limited to Jews, of course. The Japanese have a rising sun on their flag. The British once sang "Rule Britannia" with a firm conviction that their civilization was divinely destined to conquer the earth. The United States has always seen itself as being an almost divinely appointed guardian and disseminator of democracy. Americans spoke of the country expanding by manifest destiny, from sea to shining sea. As Herman Melville wrote, "We Americans are the peculiar chosen people—the Israel of our time; we bear the ark of the liberties of the world." And yet none of these nations was ever hated for its claims to chosenness, mostly because no one ever took them as seriously as those of the Jews.

What does it mean to be chosen? To be chosen is to have your uniqueness established, to be rendered special. That's why romantic love is more important to us than parental love. Our parents love us infinitely. They feed us and clothe us. They tell us we're the smartest in the class, the prettiest in the whole grade. So why would we tire of that kind of smothering love? Because our parents can do everything for us except one thing. They can't *choose* us. As such, their love doesn't make us feel special. But when someone who is not related to us, someone who has no genetic compulsion to love us, chooses us and makes us theirs, we feel infinitely precious. We live in an age where marriage is under assault, but studies show that about 80 percent of college students want to marry. We all want someone to choose us and, in the process, deselect everyone else. We want to be someone's one and only. It's part of our G-dly instinct. G-d is the one and only, and we want to be the one and only. We're created in His image.

How is chosenness practiced as a value? Simple. We're put on this earth to make each and every person feel chosen. Think about it. Chosenness invites an interaction between two people. You can never choose yourself. You depend on someone else to choose you. Now you see why marriage is a holy institution. When you ask someone to marry you, you lend them a G-dly quality. You establish their infinite worth. But there are more subtle ways to choose someone. Every time you compliment a friend, you make her feel chosen. You singled her out for praise. Every time you comfort someone in need, you have chosen him. You have identified him as worthy of your time and love.

I have a policy of trying to give a dollar to anyone on the street who asks, not because I think it will solve their problems—what can you do with a dollar?—but because if I were to ignore them and keep on walking, I would be demonstrating that there is nothing chosen about them. They are utterly ordinary. They do not even merit a moment of my time. Heck, they don't even exist. But if you take a moment and give someone a small gift, you are choosing them. You are identifying that person as deserving of your love and attention. You are conferring dignity on that person at that moment, making him or her feel chosen.

The Bible rarely uses the word "chosen" in relation to the Jews as an adjective, but rather as a verb. This conveys that they were chosen for a purpose. G-d has no favorite nations. Consider, "No, for I have chosen him, that he may charge his children and his household after him to keep the way of the Lord by doing righteousness and justice; so that the Lord may bring about for Abraham what he has promised him." Or again, "Happy is the nation whose G-d is the Lord, the people whom he has chosen as his heritage." The verse makes it clear that the Jews are chosen as G-d's witnesses to other nations to make Him known. The prophet Isaiah proclaims, "Here is my servant, whom I uphold, my chosen, in whom my soul delights; I have put my spirit upon him; he will bring forth justice to the nations." Here the word "chosen" is used in the context of being G-d's servant. The Jews are chosen to serve G-d's plan for the nations of the earth to come and recognize His presence and their corresponding moral obligations.

The same idea is echoed in Isaiah: "You are my witnesses, says the Lord, and my servant whom I have chosen." And yet again: "For I give water in the wilderness, rivers in the desert, to give drink to my chosen people, the people whom I formed for myself so that they might declare my praise." All these verses attest that Jews are chosen as ambassadors of ethical monotheism rather than as a special race that possesses intrinsic superiority to the other nations of the world. In fact, the Bible expressly dismisses racial superiority of the Jews: "Are you not as the children of Ethiopia to me, children of Israel?"

To the question of whether Jews are guilty of arrogant pretensions to racial or spiritual superiority—do they really believe themselves to be closer to G-d? The answer is no. Chosenness implies greater responsibility, with penalties as well as rewards. "You only have I singled out of all the families of the earth; therefore I will visit upon you all your iniquities." The choice of the children of Israel as G-d's people was not because of their power or merit. Far from it. It is a humbling device. As Dennis Prager and Joseph Telushkin write in *Why the Jews?* the Jews were chosen "simply because they are the offspring of the first ethical monotheist, Abraham. That is their single merit."

What gets in the way of truly appreciating chosenness are misguided contemporary ideas of homogeneity. But consider this story of Moses:

For over two hundred years the Jews were enslaved to the mighty empire of Egypt. The Almighty searched for a strong leader to deliver them. He would have to be noble, so the Jews would respect him; compassionate, so the Jews would esteem him; charismatic, so the Jews would follow him; and wise, so he could serve as an intermediary between the Jews and G-d. But according to Jewish lore, the selection of Moses was not based on his possession of any of these virtues. Instead Moses, serving as shepherd for his father-in-law, Jethro, one day was bringing the flock back from pasture and noticed that a small sheep had been left behind by the stronger, faster sheep. Moses temporarily abandoned the flock and returned to gather in the straggler. It was at that moment that the Almighty declared, "This man shall be the leader of my people," and revealed Himself to Moses as the burning bush.

The story seems to indicate that it was Moses's care for each individual that found favor in G-d's eyes. But only a fool would have risked an entire flock for the sake of a single sheep. Even worse, Moses did not return for just any sheep, but for the smallest and weakest. It was not because he believed that the straggler, if properly fed and cared for, could grow to be the pride of the flock, that he collected it. Even this small sheep was an indispensable member of the flock. Moses recognized that without this straggler the entire flock was flawed and deficient.

In other words, the secret behind this seemingly straightforward story is that Moses did not return for the sake of the straggler, but for the sake *of the flock*. Moses was, in the words of the Zohar, a *raayah mehemna*, a "trusted shepherd." He had been entrusted with an entire flock, which included the little sheep, not a collection of individuals. Had he returned from the pasture without the little sheep, he would not have brought back that with which he had been entrusted. Even replacing this sheep with another would not have served to compensate for its loss.

There is a profound lesson in this simple story. The Almighty desired a leader who knew that without every member's participation and contribution, the nation would be deficient. He wanted a leader who saw that the diversity inherent among nations, people, animals, and things—be they grand or small—was a blessing that made for a more colorful and robust whole.

In today's society people pride themselves on their tolerance. They believe they have progressed beyond the prejudices of the past. They have learned to allow opinions that do not necessarily accord with their own. Personally, I find this definition of tolerance repugnant. Rather than find enrichment or redemption in another's differences, one simply tolerates them. One swallows hard and stomachs another's right to be different. This is hardly recognizing the virtue that can be extracted from another party's distinctiveness. This is essentially a philosophy of segregation rather than a multi-ethnic society.

Tolerating another person implies that while you may not mind hearing what this person has to say today, if he were to disappear tomorrow, you would hardly notice or care. There is nothing to be learned from his conflicting opinion or uniqueness, and his absence in no way compromises or impairs one's own state of completion.

Promoting the modern definition of tolerance is really a license to indifference. It is not a call to harmony or multicultural enhancement.

Imagine a country in which all are pacifists. How long could it last? Would it not fall prey to a belligerent neighbor? Conversely, imagine a country in which all are hawks. What would prevent them from crossing the line of legitimate defense to illegitimate aggression? There is an inherent beauty in the divergence of human opinion. America today is bitterly divided between liberals and conservatives, each insistent that the other is destroying the country. How incredible that few on either side understand not just the balance found in opposing philosophies but the completion that comes from integrating the two. But to manifest the beauty of orchestrating opposing poles, one must go beyond tolerating one's colleagues, and even one's rivals, toward realizing that it is their existence and differences that allow us to maintain our own identity. Like Moses, we must adopt a communal perspective.

The country's current political stalemate is a result not of conflicting views, but rather a lack of appreciation by both groups for the other's necessity and redeeming features. All we hear about is Right and Left, Republican and Democrat. The political divisions are painful and unnecessary. Each side demonizes the other. Why can we not learn from Moses not merely to tolerate the existence of a different sheep in our flock, but to understand why that sheep is essential for the collective? What stultifying boredom would engulf the world if we were all of the same mind or heart?

Rabbi Shneur Zalman of Liadi uses the example of a bird, which not only needs two wings to fly but also must have those wings on opposite sides. It achieves flight through antithetical propulsion. Even if the bird had two wings, but they were both on the same side, it would just flop around on its back.

The ancient sages declared, "Saving a single life is akin to saving the whole world." Why so? G-d created a complete world, in which each individual, along with his or her intrinsic differences, was crucial to its perfection. When one individual is missing, there is suddenly a gross imbalance in creation that might serve to compromise the uniqueness of each of the earth's remaining inhabitants.

Here the magnitude of murder comes into perspective. The enormity of the offense is not confined to violating the sanctity of life. One murder adversely affects the entire earth. When G-d created the world, this individual was an irreplaceable component of its perfection and equilibrium. The murderer chose to disrupt that fine-tuning and throw the world into imbalance. Murder is thus the ultimate statement of arrogance. It is one man's actualization of his belief that another man serves no purpose. It is one man's arrogant affirmation that his view of life supersedes that of G-d.

In sharp contrast, Jews gave the world the idea that man could reconstruct heaven on earth by ridding the world of war, hatred, famine, disease, and especially murder. All this could be achieved by submitting to G-d's authority and living life by His rules. Each nation was endowed with a special contribution to bring to the new garden, a unique fruit or plant. The Jews received a divine message as to how all these puzzle pieces could be assembled into one great whole. What a world it would be if we could absorb this message. Everyone has something to offer and no one is superfluous. Every human being is endowed with a unique gift, and once she identifies that gift she can share it with the world.

Take the three great monotheistic faiths as an example.

Christianity excels in the area of faith. Islam excels in passion. And Judaism excels in the importance of love through law. Put them all together and you get a world of hope, excitement, and justice. To be complete, the practitioners of the three world religions need one another. Maimonides ascribes a divine purpose to Christianity and Islam. He writes that both of these religions have brought the knowledge of G-d and the Messiah to distant corners of the earth, so a universal familiarity with these concepts now exists that would not have been possible without them. And he wrote these lines 850 years ago as a victim of horrific Islamic Almohad persecution.

This is significant. Who is to say that the thief, the bigot, or the Nazi doesn't make a positive contribution to his environment? Stalin approaches the community of nations and tells them that he too has a gift to contribute to the world. It's called the Gulag Archipelago. Hitler jumps in and says that his gift is Auschwitz. Any takers? Why not? Who is to say that their contributions are any less vital than our own? This is where G-d's law comes in. Ultimately, the Almighty alone can determine which contributions enhance society and which lead to its collapse. He created all nations ethnically different, and He alone knows what serves the public good. And the purpose of the Jews is to teach G-d's moral code so we can declare which human contributions are acceptable and which must be condemned. Hitler's crematoria are not gifts but abominations, because G-d commanded us not to murder. And now you begin to understand why Hitler so hated the Jews. He was trying to establish a new code of morality and ethics based on Nazi eugenics. And as G-d's chosen messengers, the Jews stood in the way.

Chosenness, far from implying any sense of Jewish superiority, conveys the idea that all members of the family of nations must work together to create heaven on earth. Each is indispensable, and none is superior to the next. The task of the Jews is to be a light unto the nations. Light is an apt metaphor because it provides guidance. It allows us to clean the room and arrange the furniture so the home becomes fit for human habitation. G-d, too, desires to reside among man. But we must first make the earth fit to be a royal residence.

The Jews have the 613 commandments of the Torah to observe. Non-Jews have the Noahide commandments, which include prohibitions against idolatry, theft, murder, adultery and incest, cruelty to animals, and blasphemy, and the responsibility to establish and maintain societies built on justice. But the extra commandments given to the Jews do not connote superiority. Two thousand years ago, well before egalitarian enlightenment would have caused the rabbis to issue apologetics, the sages of Israel went out of their way to dismiss any sense of Jewish spiritual or racial supremacy. Rather, everything depended upon a person's deeds. "Even a Gentile who studies G-d's law is equal to the Jewish High Priest," said the sages of the Talmud. Similarly, the rabbis never reserved salvation only for Jews, declaring "the righteous of all nations have a share in the World to Come." And again: "I call heaven and earth as witnesses: Any individual, whether Gentile or Jew, man or woman, servant or maid, can bring the Divine Presence upon himself in accordance with his deeds."

The Jews were given far more divine commandments to serve as a buffer against the lawlessness and un-G-dliness they are bound to encounter on their journey. To remain faithful to their mission, they have to be extra vigilant. For the rooms of a house to be a comfortable 70 degrees during winter, the boiler room must be 250 degrees. So too, for the world to have the light of G-d shine upon it, those who teach the world about that light must burn with an added intensity.

Surely if the entire world were female, it would be insufferable. And if it were only male, it would be even more insufferable. The same would apply if the entire world were Jewish. If all people inhabiting the planet looked or thought the same, we would all die of boredom. The world achieves perfection through diversity. Judaism does not invite converts, because it is a fallacy to believe that one needs to be a Jew to enjoy proximity to G-d or lead a fulfilled life. The way G-d created each of us is the way in which He wishes for us to serve Him. By becoming a Jew, one might neglect to make to society the contributions he was created for. The world needs him just the way he is, which is why G-d created him that way.

To our great misfortune, we live in an age that actively seeks to obliterate difference. Stores are open seven days a week, so that there is no day of rest. Science and psychology have effectively demonstrated man's kinship with the animals. And society sends the message that we should all melt into one big indiscriminate morass. American pop culture has been exported to every nation on the planet. Everybody wants to fit in. If an individual is not confident about who he is and what he represents, if he cannot answer the important question of why his tradition should continue, then he will seek to be like everybody else. Nobody naturally likes being different. It takes conviction to swim against the tide.

G-d commands us in the Bible to be holy. In Judaism the word "holy" means "distinct" or "removed." Something is holy by virtue of its being dissimilar, aloof, and unique. A human being becomes holy when he acts differently from animals. When a person eats without human etiquette, we say he behaves like an animal. His human uniqueness is no longer on display. G-d is holy because He is not like man. He has no body or other corporal limitation. The Sabbath is holy because it is different from the other days of the week. To treat it like any other day is to desecrate its holiness. Jewish values teach us to be sensitive to and appreciative of differences.

CHAPTER 22

Embracing the Invisible

ᴑᴑᴑᴑᴑᴑᴑᴑᴑᴑᴑᴑᴑ

Happiness cannot be pursued; it can only ensue.
—VICTOR FRANKL

*The more we understand individual things, the
more we understand God.*
—SPINOZA

Modern society is addicted to artificial excitement. We live in anticipation of "the big moment." Our world prefers sex to love, money to emotional growth, and greed to spiritual hunger. Gratifying the senses has become a cherished goal. The result, of course, is rapid burnout. We sit at home and let DVDs transport us into a world of fantasy and adventure. People have forgotten how to be engaged by life itself.

The mystical side of Judaism teaches us how to sanctify life's seemingly insignificant moments. Kabbalah reminds us that spiritual sparks are scattered throughout the world, from the majestic mountain peaks to city slums. The infinite is omnipresent. Every time and every place can have great significance as long as we choose to inject the moment with meaning.

Once, a colleague apologized to Albert Einstein for keeping him waiting on a bridge. "You didn't keep me waiting," Einstein said. "I was standing here and working."

G-d's words to the Jewish people in uttering the first of the Ten Commandments—"I am the Lord your G-d who has taken you out from Egypt"—constituted an extraordinary demand. Until that time, all humanity worshipped tangible items grasped by the senses, such as the sun and the moon, both of which provided instant comfort and benefits. Commanding men to devote all their energies to an invisible G-d was a radical concept. No human eye could behold and no mind could conceive of the Almighty. The Jewish G-d transcends all description.

Our conception of G-d conditions us to see the subtle within the obvious. All that is most powerful in the universe is undetectable to the senses. It can only be experienced. No one has ever seen G-d, but we experience His all-encompassing presence every day. No one has ever seen love, but we have seen its effects. No one has ever seen an atom, a nucleus, a subatomic particle, or an electrical current. We know them only by their effects. The Jewish nation was born to champion subtle and invisible qualities of the spirit over the hard-edged qualities of physical existence.

This is why Judaism passionately insists that G-d is utterly mysterious and undefined. When G-d appeared to Elijah the prophet, scripture records in 1 Kings that first "there was a great wind, so strong that it was splitting mountains and breaking rocks in pieces before the Lord, but the Lord was not in the wind; and after the wind an earthquake, but the Lord was not in the earthquake; and after the earthquake a fire, but the Lord was not in the fire; and after the fire a still small voice." In the celebrated words of Joseph Albo, a medieval Jewish philosopher, "If I knew Him, I would be Him."

The contrast with the Christian G-d is considerable. Jesus is very well defined: He has a name, he is male, and there is a record of his life and actions while on earth. In Judaism, the invisible G-d possesses no body or gender, and He transcends all emotions. G-d is the source of all life and every living creature. G-d is as close to the snail as He is to the human, equally the Creator of the star cluster spanning millions of light-years and of the gnat buzzing around a picnic table.

There was a time when men of inspired religious vision knew for certain that G-d existed. Their only question was whether *they* existed. In the presence of G-d they felt so insignificant that they asked whether their being wasn't simply an illusion. Today we have come full circle. All of us are certain that we exist, but we question daily whether G-d exists.

Modern men and women are so obsessed with their own wants and needs that they look at the external world in an entirely utilitarian way. In seeing a beautiful mountain range, they are not necessarily overcome by a feeling of awe or wonder. Their first thought is how to develop the site for their own advantage—perhaps a ski resort or summer retreat. When modern man meets someone new, his first thought is how he might exploit the new relationship to his advantage. We've turned people into "contacts." When a man meets an attractive woman, his first thought is often of how she might cater to his erotic needs.

Valuing the invisible can reintroduce people to a sense of majesty and grandeur, and a sensitivity to awe and wonder. Values can teach the modern man of technology how to appreciate rather than to manipulate. When Alexander the Great asked Diogenes whether he could do anything for him, the famed philosopher replied, "Just stand out of my light." What an incredible response. The philosopher wanted nothing the great conqueror could give him, but rather only the light to gain wisdom, by which he could discern the hidden within the revealed.

We have to promote the unseen over the seen. We have to question what's really real. It hurts me to see how physical we've all become to the detriment of the spiritual. People watch TV instead of reading a book. Husbands and wives go to movies together on a Saturday night rather than having an intimate conversation. We give our children toys rather than playing board games with them. We shop rather than attend classes. We keep choosing things that grant our senses immediate satisfaction, forgetting that real pleasure comes from delayed gratification. So not only our souls suffer, but also our bodies. A world where only hard realities prevail quickly becomes uninspiring and monotonous. Our lives need a soul. They have to be plugged into the underlying electric pulse of the universe.

Only G-d and man have infinite depth and personality, making them the two most interesting things in the universe. We tire of everything else quickly. We cannot watch even the most sensational film more than a few times, but we can have endless hours of conversation with the same person. On such days as the Sabbath, when we dedicate ourselves to cultivating human friendship and human company and enhancing our relationship with G-d, we cultivate that most important of all personality traits: depth.

Jewish values are the still, small voice that whispers in the ear of the man obsessed with golf that he was created for higher things, those that cannot always be smelled, touched, seen, tasted, or heard. Jewish values are the thunder of conscience that pierces a woman's heart when she goes on a shopping spree after giving a hungry man just a few coins. Jewish values are the soothing rain that quenches the fire of selfish and competitive anger. Jewish values are about making the ordinary extraordinary, the natural miraculous, and the everyday unique.

CONCLUSION

Renewal

∞∞∞∞∞∞∞∞∞∞∞

*I believe that in the history of art and of thought
there has always been at every living moment of
culture a "will to renewal."*
—EUGÈNE IONESCO

*So as long as a person is capable of self-renewal,
they are a living being.*
—HENRI-FRÉDÉRIC AMIEL

E very life form and every relationship is constantly challenged by ob-
solescence and the stultifying, soul-draining effects of routine. Identities, too, are fragile. If a movie star continues to play the same role in
film after film, his or her fans will eventually avert their eyes. Likewise, a
comedian who repeatedly tells the same jokes, or a salesman who hawks
only one product year in and year out, will lose both audience and business. The same is true in relationships. If a husband and wife settle for
routine in their marriage, their union will grow stale and they will slowly
drift apart.

Civilizations, too, need to stay vigilant. The Roman Empire once covered seven-eighths of the civilized world. Its emperors enjoyed power beyond human imagination and its citizens benefited from a lifestyle that offered 215 holidays per year. Most work was done by slaves and its power lasted a millennium. But today all that remains of the empire are ruins. Similarly, the British Empire once ruled 25 percent of the world's landmass but forfeited its global influence to the United States.

What led to their collapse? They were defeated by the challenge of renewal. Like the dinosaurs before them, they failed to adapt to a changing world. Stagnation leads to decay. Societies that fail to renew themselves ultimately collapse. Internecine warfare made the Romans incapable of preventing their barbarian neighbors from invading, and the British failed to foresee the world transition from aristocracy to meritocracy.

But why must *we* renew ourselves? Why can't we just remain the same? When it comes to civilizations and comedy routines, we understand why renewal is essential. And if birds don't fly south for the winter, their wings freeze and they fall prey to predators. If a Muscovite wears his thick Russian bearskin in the summer, he will suffer heatstroke. But what about those of us who live in the same environment day in and day out? If things went well last year, and there are no social or environmental changes, why should we change? Why adapt if there is no external reason to do so?

Because G-d created man in His image. Just as G-d is a creator, so is man, and the nature of a creator is to remain inventive. We cannot just continue to do the same thing, because a lack of inventiveness leaves buried our deepest selves. Each and every one of us is an artist. We need to build. We are naturally businessmen, not night watchmen. It is not enough to safeguard what exists. We must expand and construct constantly. And if we're given something only to preserve, instead of build, then like the night watchman, we quickly fall asleep on the job.

The reason we must always change, adapt, and evolve is not to conform with external modifications, but rather with internal ones. As G-dly creatures, our truest, innermost selves aim for creativity.

In the same way that there are seasons of the sun, there are seasons of the soul. Man is a dynamic creature. The soul is a burning flame that flickers constantly. Man cannot stagnate on the outside, because he does not stagnate on the inside. Renewal is the key to survival and passion in all realms of life.

Every year the Jewish nation is confronted with the challenge of personal and national renewal, and this is the essence of Rosh Hashanah, the Jewish New Year, in which individuals are challenged to bring themselves forward a year to remain current. What's at risk in failing to heed the call is not merely failing to repent and failing in G-d's judgment. Rather, what we lose is the opportunity to be more passionate about everything we will do in the coming year.

The key words of the High Holy Day prayer liturgy are *teshuva, tefilla,* and *tzedaka,* or repentance, prayer, and charity. These three words capture the essence of renewal, which involves first repentance, or reaching more deeply into ourselves. Every person possesses an inner innocence, a layer of pristine purity, that can never be tarnished or compromised. Our ability to tap into this reservoir of simplicity and guiltlessness leads to real repentance. In Judaism, "teshuva" translates not as "repentance" but as "return." We are returning to our pristine, primordial selves, to our innermost essence, our true identity, which is the spark of G-d that animates us. Teshuva, then, is man reaching into himself for resurrection and regeneration.

Next is tefilla, or prayer, whereby man cries out to G-d, the source of his salvation. Prayer represents the ladder that connects G-d and man, and bridges the infinite chasm that separates mortals from the unknowable G-d.

Then there is tzedaka, or charity, wherein we reach out to our fellow man. Now that we have tapped our innocence and joined in sanctity with our source and Creator, we are able and indeed obligated to share that bounty and blessing with our fellow creatures and to experience collective salvation.

Because the final step of renewal is to find G-d in every aspect of creation, above all else, we find renewal in our compassion. Rabbi Mordechai Brody was a leading light of nineteenth-century Eastern European Jewry. He and his wife employed a young orphan girl to help with household chores. Once while the girl washed an expensive vase, she accidentally broke it. The rabbi's wife was incensed. "How can you have done something so foolish?" she yelled. "You have just broken our most expensive possession, and I cannot overlook it. Half the cost will be deducted from your pay." And with this the rabbi's wife told her husband she was going to the local Jewish court to report what had happened so the court would support her decision to hold the girl responsible for her negligence.

The aged rabbi rose and put on his heavy winter coat. "No, Mordechai, stay where you are. You do not have to accompany me outside. I shall go myself."

"Accompany you?" the rabbi asked. "No, dear, you misunderstand. I am not accompanying you. I am going to the court to represent the poor orphan girl in court."

When man reaches within, to the depths of his soul, and reaches heavenward toward the Creator, he is simultaneously overwhelmed by a feeling of G-d's abundant presence, which humbles him, and able to reach out to all his human brothers and sisters as equals. When we speak of a man or woman of greatness, we refer primarily to someone who doesn't rely on outward trappings of status, since life for him or her is an endless challenge, rich with new horizons, opportunities for enlightenment, and the incomparable joy of benefiting others. His or her life is a testament to renewal.

Renewal is never easy. It involves careful balancing. One must renew oneself without becoming totally new and unidentifiable. So one must first identify one's own irreducible essence, answering the question, "What makes me, me?" If individuals change completely—if they clear out the very features of their souls and adopt identities wholly alien to their previous selves—then they are often even worse off than before. If a man's wife cannot recognize him, she will not wish to remain married to him. The task in every act of renewal is to identify our immutable essence, then to seek to reveal it in a refreshing and passionate manner without compromising our core.

Our society today desperately needs a global Rosh Hashanah. Our personal lives do as well. We need to hear a call for renewal and respond to our inner need to re-create ourselves anew. We need to find new passion and new commitment. We dare not stagnate and go quietly into that dark night of lost potential, materialism, soullessness, and loneliness.

Jewish values, with their moral foundation and call to ethical excellence, can inspire modern men and women who long for a spirituality that will make them better people—teaching them how to be more happily married, raise more secure children, channel their ambition into purposeful actions, and transform the world into a kinder, gentler place.

Jewish values offer a program for perpetual renewal. They have largely shaped the world we inhabit, a world that now cries out for passion, inspiration, and leadership. The light of Jewish values is finally being granted an opportunity to shine openly beyond the confines of the Jewish community. May its rays illuminate the distant corners of the earth as well as the small crevices of the human heart.

ACKNOWLEDGMENTS

In writing a book on values that lead to personal and professional renewal, I have to first thank all who have educated and taught me from the time I was a boy. The names are too many to list here, but the standouts are my parents, Yoav Boteach and Eleanor Paul, who taught and modeled for me everything that is valuable in life from the very beginning; my grandparents, and especially my grandmothers, Ida Paul and Eshrat Boteach, who were largely responsible for my early formal Jewish education; my brothers and sisters, whose personal example of constant selflessness always taught me goodness; Rabbi Shneur Zalman Fellig, who inspired me to become more religious and ultimately a rabbi; Rabbi Manis Friedman, whose lectures deepened my understanding of Jewish mystical thought; Dennis Prager, my dear friend who made me so passionate about Jewish values; all the teachers I had in school and yeshiva, the most important standout of whom was the head of my academy in Jerusalem, Rabbi Asher Lemel Cohen. And most important of all, I have a lifelong debt of gratitude to my spiritual mentor and guide, the Lubavitcher Rebbe, Rabbi Menachem Mendel Schneerson, of blessed memory, who electrified the world with his scholarly orations, inspired righteousness, and world leadership of the Chabad movement.

Looking at my children often makes me weak because I feel regret for any and all errors I have made in raising them. But when it comes to finding what's really important in life, there it is, staring at you in the flesh. Thank you, Mushki, Chana, Shterny, Mendy, Shaina, Baba, Yosef, Dovid Chaim, and Cheftziba for the light you bring to my life. I also thank my brothers and sisters for being my best friends and confidants.

This book was expertly edited by Megan Hustad, who is a master at cutting away the fat (my books lean toward obesity), getting to the heart of the argument, and finding the perfect order for a compelling and entertaining read. Megan is also a scholarly woman of depth and insight.

John Sherer, the black-belt publisher of Basic Books, encouraged this project from the outset and showed consistently wise judgment. I am grateful for his confidence in me and his tendency to nearly always make the right decision.

My work colleagues are my friends and confidants, beginning with Jason Kitchen, Dean Bigbee, and Kennia Ramirez. Without their dedication, I would have little time to write.

My wife, Debbie, occupies pride of place in all my book acknowledgments. This is not a knee-jerk act of thanks for a spouse. She has earned the ink. I know few people who better embody simple decency and graciousness the way Debbie does. We were blessed to marry young and she has shared my entire adult life journey. My wife is bereft of any hint of selfish ambition, her sole desire in life being to live lovingly and generously. Her daily, personal example has taught me more about values than any other presence. Her love humbles me, her devotion uplifts me. While I write about values, she lives them.

My highest thanks goes to G-d Almighty, who has always walked with me and showed me, through myriad ways, what in life is valuable. I live to never betray His permanent trust and infinite blessing.